Highway of Holiness

Highway of Holiness

Soul Journey

JUDITH LAWRENCE

RESOURCE *Publications* · Eugene, Oregon

HIGHWAY OF HOLINESS
Soul Journey

Copyright © 2011 Judith Lawrence. All rights reserved. Except for brief quotations in critical publications or reviews, no part of this book may be reproduced in any manner without prior written permission from the publisher. Write: Permissions, Wipf and Stock Publishers, 199 W. 8th Ave., Suite 3, Eugene, OR 97401.

Resource Publications
An Imprint of Wipf and Stock Publishers
199 W. 8th Ave., Suite 3
Eugene, OR 97401
www.wipfandstock.com

ISBN 13: 978-1-61097-159-1
Manufactured in the U.S.A.

Unless otherwise indicated, all Scripture quotations are taken from the *Holy Bible*, New Living Translation, copyright © 1996, 2004, Used by permission of Tyndale House Publishers, Inc., Carol Stream, Illinois 60188. All rights reserved.

All quotations from previously published books are within the fair use category.

*This book is dedicated to
Helen Elaine Kirkland,
my sister and soul-comp*anion in Christ.

And when he comes . . . a great road will go through that once deserted land. It will be named the Highway of Holiness.

—ISAIAH 35:5A, 8

This is what the Lord says: "Stop at the crossroads and look around. Ask for the old, godly way, and walk in it. Travel its path, and you will find rest for your souls."

—JEREMIAH 6:16A

Contents

Foreword xi
Introduction xiii

1. Awareness of Our Spiritual Pilgrimage 1
2. Pilgrimage Process 15
3. Starting Our Spiritual Journey 33
4. Meeting Others on the Journey 51
5. Walking through Darkness and Light 64
6. Expect Hills and Valleys, Rivers and Deserts 77
7. Finding Open Doors Along the Way 91
8. Continuing on the Soul Journey 104

Post-Script 113
Bibliography 115

Foreword

I REMEMBER once reading that there are hard chair books and soft chair books. Highway of Holiness begins as a soft chair book and becomes one for a hard chair. Far from being a criticism, I mean this as a compliment.

To use an image that runs through the book, this book invites one to a journey that begins in simplicities—helpful and necessary simplicities—and moves into the highlands of spirituality where the air is more bracing, the slopes steeper, and the climbing more challenging.

All of which is to say that this is a call to a level of mature Christian spirituality. The depth of that maturity can be discerned in what the reader is being invited to become, nothing less than what the author calls "a contemplative without a cloister". Since contemplation, a spiritual discipline even beyond that of meditation, is perhaps the highest level of our seeking a sense of the presence of God, the reader must decide to what extent this is possible for him or her in the frantic and oppressive culture we live in.

At one point we are reminded of the Celtic tradition and its ability to retain a sense of the divine in even the most mundane activities of every day life. Again the reader has to explore the extraordinary spiritual facility of that long ago island world—and the author supplies some beautiful examples—before setting out to discover to what extent this closeness to the divine can be lived out today.

There are moments of lyrical writing, too many to include in this short expression of appreciation. Usually they come when the author is addressing us from a higher point on the spiritual ascent than many of us have attained, myself included. To say this is to be

Foreword

neither critical nor envious. The simple truth is that all of us who climb the hills of holiness stand on our own ledge or crag or minor peak, wishing to help those below us in the climb and taking heart from those who have climbed higher.

And so to two of those lyrical moments.

The first, a thought about prayer: "Prayer is the staying power that enables us to be always at one with God—God focused; one-souled with God; one-hearted with God; one-minded with God. As God desires to be with us, at one with us, so we would be at one with God."

The second is where the author ends by repeating something she said to us in her introduction to the book, in fact something that is at the heart of her understanding of the spiritual journey. This journey, she writes, "runs parallel to the journey of the physical, intellectual, and emotional. It moves more slowly and at times intertwines with it. The body, mind and ego run headlong towards their peak and, having arrived at the glory years, they sit there waiting for the end of time, perhaps declining into memories of what once was. The spiritual journey paces itself, steadily moving forward, knowing that time is on its side. In fact the spiritual way is timeless, continuing on . . . going forward . . . into eternity."

Herbert O'Driscoll

Herbert O'Driscoll has written many popular books on the spiritual life, including Portrait of a Woman; he is a sought after speaker who has traveled widely through North America, Europe, and the Holy Land. He now lives in Victoria, B.C., Canada.

Introduction

A SPIRITUAL pilgrimage begins with one step. The pilgrimage we are on is one of holiness. The first step is taken in love and faith. The first step we make requires that we step across the threshold from the place where we are now and into the unknown.

While we are on earth we are going along a physical, intellectual, emotional, and spiritual pilgrimage. As we proceed along the journey of life our bodies first gain strength until they peak then gradually break down towards the end of life; our mental faculties, too, gain knowledge until, later in life, our memories weaken and our knowledge fades away.

Our spiritual lives, however, become stronger even at the end of our physical lives because our souls go on living in the next life, the life after death, where we will live in the spirit. It is our souls that do the walking on this spiritual journey, this Highway of Holiness.

It is important for us to grow in the spirit—in love, peace, and patience—in all the fruits of the spirit as described by St. Paul in his letter to the Galatians 5:22–23. The harvest of spiritual maturity is the goal of our sacred pilgrimage, our soul journey. Our sole purpose in this life is to unite with our soul purpose and journey on the path toward holiness.

There are earthly pilgrimages, also, that can assist us on our spiritual journey. They usually have some religious significance and may give us new understanding into the life of Christ or of the saints. Earthly pilgrimages are taken for a specific length of time—they have a beginning and a goal or destination. They are often linked to our spiritual pilgrimage and give us some insight into our spiritual development. We may take several earthly pilgrimages in our lifetime; for instance we may go to Oberammergau, to the shrine of a saint, or to the Holy Land.

Introduction

Some people may walk a labyrinth in lieu of going to an actual pilgrimage site. Labyrinths came into existence in medieval times when the Church had made pilgrimages obligatory for all Christians, but it had become too dangerous to undertake them due to violent thieves along the roads where pilgrims walked. Walking the labyrinth as a spiritual exercise is again becoming popular in the twenty-first century and there are many places and meditation centers where they can be found.

A spiritual pilgrimage is ongoing. It is the pilgrimage of the soul and we may not be aware that it is happening at first. From time to time, we may get some holy intuition of this pilgrimage and, as we mature, we become more in tune with the soul's journey. We begin the spiritual pilgrimage in holiness, we walk the Highway of Holiness, and the goal is holiness.

The journey begins when we are born and goes on throughout our earthly life and even into our life after death. God is at the starting line with us; God is with us on our path; and God is at the finishing line.

> Let us run with endurance the race God has set before us. We do this by keeping our eyes on Jesus, the champion who initiates and perfects our faith. (Heb 12:1b–2a)

When we go across the threshold and out through the gate, which is Christ, we proceed along our path to holiness, growing in spiritual maturity until we reach the highest sanctity we can achieve on earth. Whether we are on a spiritual back road, foot path, or paved highway, if we are searching for a closer relationship with God, we are on the Highway of Holiness.

Each one of us has to run his or her spiritual race on the road of life. It is not how fast one arrives at the finish line that matters but that one continues steadily forward. For the Christian, Jesus is the author or pioneer of our journey, the one who goes before us. Jesus breaks new ground, draws the map, and guides us on our way. Jesus walks with us and when we reach the end of our earthly course greets us, washes us, anoints us and crowns us with

Introduction

the laurel-wreath. Jesus proclaims our arrival to be perfect in the name of Christ. We persevere through all things and arrive at the end of the earthly journey in Christ's triumph.

Christ runs the race and walks the pilgrimage with us; Christ is continually by our side. Christ encourages us, gives us the water of life and daily nourishment for the journey. Christ is there at the beginning—Alpha; and is there at the end—Omega. Christ is Author and Finisher; Christ is Pioneer and Perfecter.

It is the soul that walks our spiritual journey; it is the soul that is holy from the time before we were born; it is the soul that remains our core of holiness throughout our life on earth; it is the soul that re-enters heaven in holiness, having matured and expanded through our spiritual pilgrimage.

This book will assist you on your spiritual journey; it will guide you in prayer and a deepening relationship with God; it will show you the difference in the development of the various parts of your being—body, mind, ego, spirit, and soul.

You will see how each person's spiritual journey is unique yet equally valid as that of others who are on the soul pilgrimage. You will see how you are able to help others on the Highway of Holiness even though your soul journey may differ from theirs.

You will take a look at the difficulties and joys along the way and how God is with you at all times; you will learn to recognize God's open doors and unexpected miracles along the way. You will be enabled to live a fear-free life in God's love.

On your journey, you will learn to listen to the voice of your soul and your soul will strengthen its qualities and assist you in finding your unique relationship with God. As the soles of your feet walk the physical road of your life so the soul of your being walks the Highway of Holiness and directs your growth in spiritual maturity.

I pray that your soul qualities will continue to develop and the fruits of your spirit will grow and mature along your sacred journey of life.

1

Awareness of Our Spiritual Pilgrimage

SPIRITUAL EXPLORATION

As human beings we have a sense of longing within us. At first, we do not understand that this innate longing is from the soul. We search for fulfillment, we search for something that we feel we need to make us complete. We may presume, especially when we are younger, that we are looking for the perfect mate so that we will be a perfect couple and later a family. This is part of our earthly, physical pilgrimage and it is the way in which most of us, though not all, travel through our lives.

As we get older, whether we are married or not, we begin to be aware of our spiritual side and our soul starts to make itself known; or perhaps it is that we become more attuned to the soul within and begin to listen to its voice. We are aware of a desire within us to come to know God at a deeper level and our spiritual pilgrimage begins in earnest. We are all longing for something; and we are all seeking that for which we long. We must open ourselves up to the Holy Spirit in order to discover our personal spiritual path.

Do you feel as if you have been brought to the edge of possibility, that here before you lies your new spiritual day, the day that is the expression and discovery of God's Spirit within you? This is your soul making itself heard, beckoning you on. You are about to take the next step in your spiritual journey. You will not know what lies ahead of you but you can be sure that God will keep you safe whatever comes for it is through God's calling that your spiritual journey is mapped out for you.

Allow yourself to be open to God's newness of spirit in you; open yourself to the next stage of your spiritual exploration. Accept the gift of new life from God, whatever it may be. Look to God and be totally confident that all will be well. You have no idea of what is to happen but you can feel quiet and confident in God's Holy Spirit. There will be pitfalls but God will hold you safe. Rely on God and be open to the leading of the Sacred One. Look for guidance from your soul.

Today is the first day of your new life in God. The new vision that God has for you will be unbelievable, at times overwhelming, and always truly wonderful. You are on your spiritual pilgrimage; you will have the journey of your life on this Highway of Holiness. Hold on tight to God's hand and enjoy each moment.

PILGRIMS

> What joy for those whose strength comes from the Lord, who have set their minds on a pilgrimage to Jerusalem. (Ps 84:5)

A pilgrim is one who journeys to a sacred place or a future life. Those of us who are set on this journeying process towards a sacred place are joyful. When we walk with God we discover that the journey and the arrival are one and the same; being on the journey and arriving at the journey's end is one and the same moment in time. God is the journey and its arrival; God is the path and the attainment of its goal. Our home is in God and our journey is with God.

We are all pilgrims on life's road. What is the modern day pilgrim seeking? What are you seeking? What is God seeking from us? God desires that we come to know the Lord's love for us and that we understand that God's love is within us; we are to love God and ourselves, and to share God's love with others.

Awareness of Our Spiritual Pilgrimage

There may be times on your journey when you wonder why you are in a particular place; you may wonder why you would have chosen to work in such an odd line of work or such an out of the way part of the country. God is the reason you are there and you may never know what that reason is. You are there because God needs to be there and God has chosen to be there through you. When God asks you to help someone, you must try to be generous; if God needs you to receive from someone, you must try to be appreciative of that person's generosity, remembering that the gift is from God.

At times on the journey we will need a drink of water and at other times God will ask us to provide a drink of water for someone else. We should take what is offered with thanksgiving. We must not be choosy from whom we will receive a gift, nor be selective of the person who will receive the cup of water from our hands. We should give to and receive from the one who is present to us now and the cup will be replenished for the next person. If we wait for another opportunity to give or receive the offering, the water will evaporate or spill and the cup will become empty. We shouldn't wait for some future moment to do the job that needs to be done; the journey is now, the joy is now.

NEEDS OF A SPIRITUAL PILGRIM

If we are going on a physical pilgrimage we will likely plan ahead. We would need a place to stay overnight; we would need a map; we would pack a bag with traveling necessities.

The spiritual pilgrim also has traveling needs.

Daily Quiet Time and Place

Every day of your life you are on a spiritual pilgrimage and every day of your life you need to spend preparation time with God for the strength needed for your journey.

One of the most important requirements of the spiritual pilgrim is a daily quiet time and place. In order to focus fully on God throughout your spiritual pilgrimage you need to put aside time each day for quiet prayer and meditation. This daily time is where you get rest and renewal for the coming day's journey toward spiritual maturity.

The scriptures tell us that God indwells us (1 John 2:27; 4:13, 15, 16) and now, in this quiet time of meditation, in this time of silence and stillness, we reinforce the truth of the promise of these words and come to understand the meaning Christ's words have for us in our daily life. During our quiet time, the mind's knowing becomes the soul's reality as we begin to understand the meaning of the words, "For in [God] we live and move and exist" (Acts 17:28a).

Through the day it is difficult to hear God's voice with all that is going on around you. Having a daily quiet time will assist you to become more attuned to hearing God's voice and seeing the Sacred One in your surroundings throughout the day. In your quiet time you grow more open to hearing God's voice and so your ability to see and hear the Lord during the rest of the day grows also.

You will begin to see God all around you in nature, in work, at home, in family, and in other people. You will begin to live a life of gratitude, making a point of thanking God each time you notice something good that has come to you.

As you proceed along the gratitude journey you begin to be thankful, not only for joys and beautiful things, but also for sorrows and difficulties; things you once thought ugly and undesirable, you now realize can bring you closer to God.

Practice is what makes this come about and the practice begins in your quiet time and place with God each morning. As you read the scriptures and meditate on their meaning for your life; as you read other spiritual books and journal your spiritual pilgrimage; and as you pray and intercede for others, you begin to note that God seems to have a purpose for you in all that happens to you. As you discover that God has a purpose for you in this life you

Awareness of Our Spiritual Pilgrimage

discover that your soul also has a purpose; and that purpose is to help you unite with God and follow God's purpose for you.

It is in the silence that you come to be aware of God's purpose in everything you experience; it is in the morning silence that you come to grow in spiritual maturity and in gratitude for God's love and the Lord's indwelling; and it is in the early morning silence that you respond in love to God, grow in love to God, and begin to experience a mutual love between God and your soul.

HOW MUCH TIME DOES GOD NEED?

It is not how much time God needs from you that is at issue but how much time you are able and willing to give to God and to yourself to prepare for your daily spiritual pilgrimage.

At first, when you consider taking up a meditation practice or think about setting aside a time for quiet prayer, you may feel that you really don't have the time for it. Your life is already filled up with a hundred and one things to do and you know that you don't have the time to fit them all into your day as it is. How then can you possibly fit in any time for meditation? What about an hour? Impossible! How about a half-hour? Too much! Would ten minutes be possible? Well, maybe. Perhaps you could give that a try.

Would it mess up your day badly if you sit for ten minutes and say a prayer to God to guide you through your day? Would it be so difficult to take a few minutes to read the psalm and scripture readings for the day and jot down a few words that strike you as relevant to your life? At first, yes, it will be difficult to slot this time into your regular routine. It will require an adjustment to your morning hours. Are you willing to try?

You may need to get up a little earlier in order to work prayer time into your early morning routine. What can it hurt to try for a week? Before you know it, with this morning practice, you begin to find yourself less hurried in your life rather than more rushed as you thought you would be. You may want more than ten minutes and you try twenty minutes and, later, half an hour then, perhaps, even more.

Your days become less rushed and, even though the meditation time leaves you with less time to do the same amount of work, you seem to get through the tasks just the same and perhaps with more peace than before.

In your time of meditation and quiet with the Sacred One, you glimpse God and receive God's love and light. As a relationship with your special partner grows by being with that special person, talking with that special person, spending time quietly with that one special one, so does your relationship with God grow by making time to be with the Lord. In so doing, you grow in the Spirit; your soul expands and has more room for God's love.

The Importance of Routine

I think you will find that having a routine for your quiet time is beneficial. A routine includes such things as a set time, a set place, and a set format.

SET TIME

A set time is not an absolute must but it will prevent you from putting off your God time for no particular reason. Even if you cannot make your appointment with God—and it is not always possible—you will know that you have missed it and can judge whether it was a legitimate reason or not.

Coming to your quiet time at the same time each day is better, by far, than taking time for prayer haphazardly, when you have a moment or break in your day. Haphazard time for prayer may work out in some cases but, most often, your prayer time will suffer from a syndrome known as "But first . . . " e.g. But first, I'll put on a load of laundry; but first, I'll take out the garbage.

Pretty soon, the break in your day has been consumed by the physical things that often take precedence over spiritual matters.

Jobs of a physical nature tend to take priority because they are tangible and measurable whereas spiritual activities that are unseen may appear less important or even convict you falsely of laziness because you have no visible proof that you were doing anything of value. A pile of clean, folded laundry or a stack of washed dishes gives validation to the work you have done; you have visible, tangible evidence that you did something of value. What evidence can you show that prayers have been prayed or scriptures read? You have to have faith in God and your soul that this spiritual work is of value to God, your soul, and to others.

Set Place

If it is possible, a set place for your quiet time is also good though, again, not an absolute necessity. Many people do not have the luxury of a spare room, an unused corner, or closet. But, look around you, be creative—perhaps you could find a small area in some corner of your home where you could place a chair and side table and cordon them off with a screen.

This will give you a place to leave your spiritual paraphernalia—your prayer books, reading material, Bible, and journal; candles, rosary, or other religious icons and imagery that you might use. It will be a place where you can return day after day; a place where a prayerful atmosphere and spiritual presence will be built up. This will be a place where you can continue tomorrow where you leave off today; this is a place that welcomes you and to which you look forward to returning.

You can, of course, pray anywhere. Christ was an itinerant preacher and must have had many places where he practiced alone-time with the Father. However, the Mount of Olives is a place where Christ went to pray—a place mentioned in the Gospels, which seemed to have a strong pull for the Lord. If you can find a special prayer place, follow Christ's example and go there regularly—make it a customary daily exercise of joy, strength, and communion with God.

HIGHWAY OF HOLINESS

Set Plan

Now that you have set up a scheduled time and place to be with God you might very well say that you haven't the least idea of how to get started. You might wonder if there is some outline that you can follow to make the most of this daily quiet time. You might ask if there is some plan that *has* to be followed to make your time of meditation work for you.

You may think that you are being too presumptuous to consider making time for a relationship with God. You may say, "I'm not a saint, what right do I have to expect God to take time to listen to what I have to say, or for God to desire to be with me and speak to me?" There is no doubt that God wants to be with each one of us—the Lord loves you and me, and desires that we should each grow in our desire to be with the Sacred One.

Let us take a look at some of the practical points that can help you as you begin your meditation practice. What should you do when you come to this special time and place of aloneness with God? How do you meditate and commune with God? What is the purpose of this time? Each person has a unique relationship with God so the answers to the above questions are as many and as different as the number of individuals who read this book.

However, when you first begin, it can be useful to have a structure that you can follow if you so desire; but you should know that there is no right and wrong way to go about your quiet time in which to develop a relationship with God. Let the Holy Spirit lead you; open yourself to listen to God's guidance as you go through your quiet time. Speak to God as you would with a friend, or just sit quietly in God's loving presence.

> My heart has heard you say, "Come and talk with me." And my heart responds, "Lord, I am coming." (Ps 27:8)

Possible Outline

Quieting Down Time

When I come to my morning quiet time I have already done quite a lot of things; my mind is busy with many thoughts and I need to come to stillness and peace; I need to gather myself into a prayer mood or prayer spirit.

In order to do this, I read a few short words of a mystical or spiritual nature. I often choose words from Julian of Norwich, a fourteenth century mystic from England, Lalla, a fourteenth century poet and mystic from India, or others who express their love for God through nature.

By the time I have done this my mind, heart, and soul are linked to God and I am ready to commune with the Sacred One—speak to God and hear what the Lord has to say to me.

There are other ways to bring yourself into a prayer mood; you could light a candle, play some music conducive to prayer, or say a prayer of praise to God. It is the routine that is important so that the soul knows now you are ready to be with God.

Psalm and Scripture Readings

Personally, I follow the order of Bible readings and psalms as laid out in the Canadian Anglican Church lectionary. There are, of course, other sources for daily psalm and scripture readings or you can follow your own method of going through the books of the Bible. I like to have a reading from the book of Psalms, the Old Testament, one of the four Gospels, and one of the other New Testament books. The advantage of following a lectionary is that the various readings are linked together in a theme, the seasons of the church year are given emphasis, and the feast days of the saints may be given special remembrance and readings.

As you read the scriptures, sometimes words will jump out at you as being meaningful to your life. When that happens, it is best to stop right then and write down the passage in your notebook. Don't make the mistake of saying that you will go back at the end of your readings and write them out. If you do that, often the words that you thought were so important, will have become elusive, hidden among the other words and you will have lost the chance to meditate on these special thoughts.

Spiritual Reading

After the readings from the Bible, I usually read from a spiritual reading book. This is a book that guides me on my spiritual path, helps me to grow in spiritual maturity, and brings me closer to God. Here, too, if any words seem to have special significance in my life, I jot them down in my notebook, making sure that I name their source, author, and page number. This ensures that if I want to make reference to them at a later date I will know exactly where to find them.

I have some favorite books that I return to many times gaining new insight each time I read them. Not all my spiritual reading books are in the Christian tradition—other religions have good things to offer and can assist us in our spiritual growth. One needs to keep an open mind and search for God-truths in all kinds of places.

Meditation

When you have finished your readings, return to your notebook and read over any words you have written down and begin your time of meditation.

First, say a prayer to God asking the Holy Spirit to show you what God wants you to discover; ask that your mind, heart, and soul be open to God so that you can hear what the Holy Spirit wants you to learn.

Meditation can take many forms. Basically, it is a way to become closer to God, to know God's love for you, and to deepen

Awareness of Our Spiritual Pilgrimage

your love for God. You can journal, you can think about how God relates to your life, or you can think about the words you took from your readings.

My preferred way of meditation is journaling. I just keep writing whatever comes into my mind about God, about the quotations from my earlier reading, or about how God guides me in my daily life. Journaling has the advantage for me in that my thoughts don't become so distracted, they stay more on track, or can be more easily brought back on track if they wander—that track being God.

I think that one of the best descriptions of meditative journaling that I have found is one given by Christina Baldwin. She says, "The comfort that comes from questioning is this: even if there isn't an answer, there *is* a response. There is a sense of the sacred reaching toward us, as we reach toward it. And the most tangible evidence of this mutuality often occurs in the journal, in dialogues and insight and the reflections of the writing process. The voice of the sacred appears gently on the page, written in our own handwriting but carrying a message of support and comfort, sometimes challenge, which we do not generate alone."[1]

Journaling is a seeking of the Sacred One on our part and a message from the Sacred One on the part of the divine. The message may be one of encouragement such as keep on searching, or seek to grow in the Spirit; it may be an assurance that you are surrounded by God's love and kindness; or it may be any one of a thousand other messages God wants to impart to you on any particular day.

If you decide to try your hand at meditative journaling just write whatever comes to mind without over-thinking it. If no spiritual thoughts seem to come, at first, it is not a cause for concern. If you continue to write, you will often find a breakthrough after about a page and a half of writing. Don't censor your thoughts, words, or grammar. This allows the Holy Spirit to flow through your soul and onto the page.

1. Baldwin, *Life's Companion*, 39.

Meditation, however you practice it, is part of your spiritual quest; it brings you closer to God and assists in your growth in the Spirit.

Contemplation

Some mornings, in your quiet time, you may be moved by the Holy Spirit to spend time in contemplation. The words meditation and contemplation are often used interchangeably but there is a difference.

Meditation involves thinking about God and God's attributes. It is a way of considering what God has done for you and what the Lord desires you to do for the Sacred One. It is a way to find out more about God and your relationship with the divine; it is an opportunity to talk and commune with one another.

Contemplation, on the other hand, does not involve thoughts or conversation. Contemplation is simply a matter of looking at God in total adoration. In contemplation you are filled up completely with your love for God. In contemplation you simply sit or kneel in God's presence and look at God with an overflowing, loving heart, and receive God's abundant love for you.

> Let all that I am wait quietly before God. (Ps 62:5a)

In bringing my whole being—all that I am—before God and waiting quietly, I can begin to see beyond surface seeing; I can begin to see with the eye of the soul. In contemplation, the eye of the soul sees beyond the surface; it sees with depth and height; in breadth and length; out to the horizon and beyond where prayer is not trapped in a box of our conformity. The eye of the soul sees with unpredictability; it sees God untamed by human images; it sees God in out of the ordinary reflections. The eye of the soul sees things in the wild, in the wilderness, and beyond the ordinary, where wild creatures, blossoms, and ideas are seen through God's amazing freedom, in all the Creator's beauty and generosity.

Awareness of Our Spiritual Pilgrimage

Though I say that contemplation does not involve words, because we are thinking beings we may still need words to bring us into a contemplative state. It is unlikely that you could come from a thinking reasoning state and enter into a gazing adoring state without some transition.

The following simple steps will help you transition into contemplation of God:

Sit comfortably with your back straight, your feet flat on the floor, your hands cupped in your lap.

Close your eyes.

Be aware of your breathing but do not seek to change it.

Say the following three phrases, in your mind or out loud, with gaps of silence between the phrases:

Let my body be still . . . still . . .

Let my breath be quiet . . . quiet . . .

Let my heart beat be steady . . . steady . . .

Continue these phrases with increasing gaps of silence until such time as your brain doesn't jump in to fill the silent gaps with thoughts.

Once you are in contemplation, just continue there as long as you are able, ending with a prayer of thanksgiving to God.

LIFE OF PRAYER

The life of prayer to which God has called us is important and should not be forgotten. We need to make a commitment to prayer. Prayer does not rely on us leaving the house, we do not have to go anywhere, or travel to other venues. Prayer can be done at home or wherever we are. We are given people for whom we are to pray and we are to bring them into the circle of our prayer life.

John O'Donahue says, "When your soul turns into a wilderness, it is the prayer of others that brings you back to the hearth of warmth. I know people who have been very ill, forsaken, and damaged; the holy travellers that we call prayers have reached out to them and returned them to healing."[2]

We do not have to make a physical journey to the people for whom we pray; we travel in thought and prayer to bring them and their needs into the circle of God.

2. O'Donahue, *Eternal Echoes*, 217.

2

Pilgrimage Process

As soon as we are born we begin to grow physically, intellectually, emotionally, and spiritually. The physical, intellectual, and emotional growth continues throughout our earthly lives until they peak and then begin to wane as we reach the end of our lives on earth. Our spiritual growth, however, is not finite and continues on into the time of our soul's rebirth into heaven and beyond.

At the end of our time on earth we no longer have need of our current physical bodies, mental faculties, and emotional natures. But our souls live on in their eternal home and are given free rein to lead our spiritual beings in continued growth until we reach full spiritual maturity and are one with the Supreme Being. Of course, I do not know how this will be achieved but, in faith, I walk the spiritual journey trusting God and my soul to lead me on my pilgrimage and bring me safely to my goal.

Every pilgrimage has a goal. The goals of earthly and physical pilgrimages may be many and varied and may include destinations, job changes, promotion within jobs, or volunteering to help others in need. The goal of a soul pilgrimage is to grow in spiritual maturity and become totally at one with God. In order to arrive at that goal we have to walk the daily pilgrimage path. We walk step by step, hour by hour, day by day, taking care to learn our spiritual lessons as they are presented to us along the way.

We give daily attention to the details that God gives us along the pilgrim way. We go with God along the journey; we arrive with God at the goal; and we realize that the journey and the goal are one and the same—the journey is God and the goal is God.

PLANTING AND HARVESTING

Jesus said, "You know the saying, 'Four months between planting and harvest.' But I say, wake up and look around. The fields are already ripe for harvest. The harvesters are paid good wages, and the fruit they harvest is people brought to eternal life. What joy awaits both the planter and the harvester alike" (John 4:35–36)!

The planting and the harvesting cannot be separated from one another; the journeying and the arrival at the journey's end are one and the same. The spiritual planting time and harvesting time have one destiny—people being brought to eternal life; the purpose of the pilgrimage process is our continued maturity in the spirit and our union with God.

Earlier, I said that we begin our physical, mental, emotional, and spiritual growth as soon as we are born. However, it may be some time before we are aware that we are on these growth paths. We will probably become aware of our physical and mental growth, and even our emotional growth, long before we realize that we each have a soul and that the soul pursues her own growth—growth in the spirit.

We become conscious of our physical growth quite early on in life. Physically, our weight and height are noted on a regular basis. We are monitored at the doctor's office; our parents clap their hands when we start to crawl then walk; and there may be a place at home where our height is measured once a year.

Intellectually, our growth is also noted at a young age. Parents brag about how far ahead we are in speech, in reading, or in drawing compared to others in our grade. We like to receive praise from our parents and teachers, and we try to do what we think will please them so that we get the pleasure of their happiness and keep in their good graces.

As far as the emotional side of our being is concerned we tend to think of it as just the way we are and not something that needs growth though, perhaps, we may think of it as a side of us that needs to be brought under control or hidden from others. For instance, we may need to get over our shyness if we want to socialize with others or control our anger if we want to get along in our jobs.

For both physical and intellectual growth there are measurable standards by which our progress can be compared. However, for spiritual growth there are no such universal standards other than those within different religions or denominations and these standards are more in the order of obedience to the laws set out in the various religious faiths.

Spiritual growth is unique to each one of us and cannot be compared to or measured alongside another's growth. God is not looking for conformity but a special, one-of-a-kind relationship with each individual.

Our spiritual growth is not the same as the development of our conscience, which alerts us to right and wrong behaviors. It is true that we do want to please God by doing the right thing, but that is similar to wanting to please our teachers and parents by working hard and getting good grades, keeping our rooms clean, or helping around the house.

Instead of allowing our thoughts, emotions, and egos to *run* our lives, we can gather together the attributes of our minds, hearts, egos, and bodies, bring them into our souls and allow them to serve in our spiritual growth. Our intellects, emotions, and physical natures are gifts from God and are not to be discarded or shunned but used with thanksgiving for the healing of the world and its growth toward holiness. During this time, we become more aware of our unique relationship with the Sacred One and our growth toward spiritual maturity.

As we go further along our spiritual journey, we will notice that our bodies, minds, emotions, and egos will strive less for superiority one over the other; they will also have less dominance over our souls and spirits. They begin to gather together in one being; they join and unite in one created, God-grown, holy being; they desire to join together in one beautiful entity that God is bringing into spiritual fruition.

The spiritual pilgrimage is the journey of the soul. At its core, the character of the soul is holiness. As we go along our spiritual path, our whole being is reaching towards holiness. It is as if at the core of our souls a spiritual seed dwells—a seed of holiness—and, as it grows, it develops into a sacred plant, flower, and fruit of holiness.

As we walk our soul journey, our spiritual growth is inevitable and does not come through quantifiable work or obedience to a particular set of religious beliefs. Our spiritual growth proceeds steadily and our souls are enabled to grow stronger because we live a disciplined spiritual life. We grow to spiritual maturity and holiness as a plant grows, produces flowers, and bears fruit.

There is no other human or spiritual being, in God's eyes, quite like each one of us. I walk God's path for me; you walk God's path for you. My relationship with the Sacred One will not be the same as your relationship with the Holy One. The flowers and fruit that develop on the plant that is my being will not be the same as yours; and the differences between my plant and yours are not cause for judgment or jealousy but for rejoicing and awe at God's amazing care, concern, and love for each one of us.

VISIBLE OUTCOMES OF JOURNEY

On the soul journey we are not looking for measured results—we are just following the path God gives us and attending to the things that come our way.

We won't always see the results of walking our journey with God; we won't always hear of how others are affected by the way we live our lives as we walk our pilgrimage. This may be difficult for us—we are hooked on praise for our good looks and physical prowess from an early age, we expect rewards for our mental accomplishments, and so it is only natural that we expect to hear that others are impressed by our spiritual maturity. The way we walk our pilgrimage *does* have results and consequences for others, whether we are aware of them or not, and the results may not always be as positive or as beneficial as we would like to believe they are.

The poet, John Masefield, in his poem, The Everlasting Mercy, says that Christ plows the furrow straight. You must walk your path and plant your field in the straight furrow that Christ plows in you, so that every moment counts whether you are aware of someone being helped or not. You have to live your life in God's love even though you can't always see the outcome of the way you walk along your pilgrim way. If you smile or say a kind word to someone and that someone doesn't respond in like manner it is not the time for you to get discouraged and think it's not worth while trying to help when you get no response or thanks. That person may have been helped by your smile more than she was able to express; your kind word may have given her the encouragement she needed to get through a very difficult day.

On the journey it is important to learn that though an immediate good result of your actions may not be apparent, a seed has been planted and has the possibility of bringing forth a harvest. In any case, you are not on this road to earn brownie points or to get a pat on the back for making someone else feel good, but rather to grow in your own spiritual maturity and to develop your relationship with God.

By the way in which you walk your journey, you may lift a burden from someone's shoulders; you may prevent someone from falling; you may refresh someone as if giving a cold drink to a thirsty person. It is possible to fulfill a person's need by the way you present yourself at any given moment along your journey, and you may never know it! Recently I was told by a woman that she had been helped by something I did thirty-five years earlier, something that eased her fear that day. When she related the event to me, I had no recollection of it—to me it had been a small thing and didn't make any impression on my memory but to her it had meant a lot.

You may be the one to break the chain of anger that started with someone's unkind word in the early morning hours and went from one person to another throughout the day. You may be the one to break the chain of hurt and start a new chain of joy by saying a word of thanks for another's work or effort, and you may never know it.

We are each responsible for our own journeying process, yet we all need to be open to opportunities to help one another along the spiritual path, even though we may never know that we were of help.

JOURNEYING IN STAGES

> Abram continued traveling south by stages toward the Negev.
> (Gen 12:9)

It was not just Abram's destination that was important but the journey. Abram didn't get to the Negev in one fell swoop. He went there by stages, stopping here and there, tarrying awhile. These people were nomadic; they traveled a certain distance then pitched their tents for a while so that their herds could rest and graze. They came at last to what seemed like their final destination. But then Abram started his journey again, retracing his steps.

Some lessons have to be repeated many times. We may think we have conquered some bad habit or learned patience in trying circumstances at work or at home, then some little thing triggers an automatic response of anger and we find the old demons surfacing, putting us back in a place we have been through all too often. We have to repeat the lesson and travel the same road; maybe this time it will be a longer space of time before we fall and have to repeat the lesson again.

> From the Negev, they continued traveling by stages toward Bethel, and they pitched their tents between Bethel and Ai, where they had camped before. (Gen 13:3)

Abram had become very rich by this time and decided to share the land with Lot, giving Lot first choice. Lot chose what seemed to be the better land and Abram took the remaining portion.

When Lot had left him, God instructed Abram to look around him to the north, south, east and west, telling him that God would give him all the land surrounding him, as far as he could see. However, it would take more than just looking at the land in order for Abram to receive it as his own. God tells Abram, "Go and walk through the land in every direction, for I am giving it to you" (Gen 13:17).

It took more than just looking at the land for Abram to receive his inheritance from God; it took walking the land, working, doing, and following God's promise. When Abram completed the journey he settled his tents in Hebron and built an altar to the Lord.

In such a way God speaks to us. God says, "Look at what is before you, rise up and walk through it and I will give it to you." God shows us eternal life and we journey on our daily pilgrimage toward it in order to claim it. God establishes and fulfills the Holy Spirit's promise when we follow God's guidance. If we say a holy "yes" to what God is offering us, it will be ratified and sanctified. Giving praise and thanks to God for what the Holy Spirit has done in our lives is our way of building an altar to the Lord.

SLOW AND STEADY JOURNEY

The journey of spiritual pilgrimage is not to be rushed. It is a slow and steady process; it is a journey that requires time—time to walk, time to stop and look, time to rest and pray, and quiet time for spiritual nourishment.

HIGHWAY OF HOLINESS

It may be some time along the spiritual way before you begin to understand that the measures used to assess your physical and mental growth cannot be applied to assess your spiritual growth. Maturity of the spirit comes as you walk the soul journey. As long as you continue your daily quiet time, your alone time with God, your growth in the spirit will happen. In your regular time of quiet, spiritual reading, and prayer, your soul is open to God's love and guidance. As you continue to receive God's love your spiritual growth happens. It is not of your *doing* but of your *receiving*—receiving God's gifts of love and grace, through which your spirituality matures.

It is in your daily spiritual practice that you begin to have an awareness of God's bountiful love within you. You begin to listen for and recognize the voice of your soul. You begin to pay attention to what your soul is telling you so that your spirit is enabled to grow and mature.

You begin to understand that Christ's home is in you; and as you begin to understand and settle into your awareness of God's love, you begin to have an inkling of how vast God's love is. You begin to *experience* this love; you begin to desire an awareness of God's loving presence always. Christ's love, present in your soul, completes you, and makes you whole and fully alive.

This is your spiritual pilgrimage—to be completely aware of Christ's presence with you always and to be filled up with the life and soul power that comes from God. Your desire to grow in awareness of God is what makes your spirit grow in maturity. The more you want to be with God, the more you are with God.

The ego voice that has spoken so loudly in your being for most of your life has more and more difficulty in making itself heard; it has less and less power over your thoughts. The gentle soul voice quietly grows in strength within your being; its roots grow down deep and long, hidden in the secret place, the ground of God's being, so that the soul flower of holy love shows itself to others—the flower that is the love of Christ. The power of the soul is the power of gentleness—gentle authority, gentle holiness, and gentle truth.

Recently, I was reading a book about the Carthusians by Nancy Klein Maguire. I came across the words where she describes the summer of Dom Philip's third year in Parkminster, the Charterhouse in West Sussex, England: "Lamentations 3: 26 echoed around the periphery of his brain: 'It is good to wait in silence for the greeting of God.'"[1]

So often, one isn't waiting for anything, in silence or otherwise. In this case, I was just sitting on the porch reading and enjoying Maguire's book, not particularly waiting for God or some holy message. I was just being myself and God appeared to me in that beautiful translation of the verse from Lamentations.

God greeted me in that little verse—jumped into my life and thoughts. God, of course, is always in our lives but, every now and again, God gives us a surprise greeting, reminding us of the divine presence always with us, "here and now," as the Carthusians say. It is like a little kiss from the Beloved. God kisses us because God loves us and desires to be with us in every moment; God greets us with little surprises for us to discover and enjoy, surprises that remind us of the divine presence within.

We do not know the hour that God will surprise us with a little love note or a greeting, nor the place where it will be found. We must always be on the look out for God's surprises and little gifts for which we have not asked and, when they come, we should enjoy them to the fullest giving God thanks for the gift, the greeting, or the kiss.

In that verse, I was brought back to myself; brought back to the knowledge that I am one with God—one with the divine. I live within God and God lives within me. It is not like living in a bubble but like dwelling within the rarefied air of the Holy Spirit. I live in this sanctified air and am made fully alive by the breath of the Holy Spirit.

1. Maguire, *Infinity Of Little Hours*, 160.

HIGHWAY OF HOLINESS

I move within this Holy Breath as if I am moving and singing in harmony with God's holy music. I sing, and dance, and make melody with the holy music of divine Spirit's love. Within the Holy Spirit I live, and move, and have my being; and, apart from the Holy Spirit, my being is not fully all it can be. When I allow myself to be in the Holy Spirit, at one with the Holy Spirit, move with the Holy Spirit, then I am all I can be. I listen to the melody of the Holy Spirit and make harmony with that melody.

I live and breathe with and in the Holy Spirit, becoming fully alive within the divine. I am one with the divine; my spirit grows, matures, and is sanctified within the divine Holy Being. I become a full blossom of praise. I sing, move, and blossom within that praise to God.

> I pray that from [the Creator's] glorious, unlimited resources he will empower you with inner strength through his Spirit. Then Christ will make his home in your hearts as you trust in him. Your roots will grow down into God's love and keep you strong. And may you have the power to understand, as all God's people should, how wide, how long, how high, and how deep his love is. May you experience the love of Christ, though it is too great to understand fully. Then you will be made complete with all the fullness of life and power that comes from God. (Eph 3:16–19)

Spiritual growth happens continuously—it is inevitable; and the fullness of that growth increases with our openness to God's love.

On the pilgrim way we learn to love whole-heartedly. Throughout our lives, since we were young, ego has taught us to disparage ourselves, others, and even God. We want others to love and respect us, yet ego is constantly whispering that we are not worthy of being loved. At the same time, ego tells us that others are unworthy of our love and respect, that they did this and that wrong, or that they didn't do as good a job on some task as we would have done.

Not only that, ego tells us that though we have been told that God is a God of love, God really is a God of power who will use that power against us, to punish us because we are unworthy of God's love—in fact, that we are unlovable.

The soul is eternal and knows differently; the soul knows that we were born in love and holiness. Ego wants to be stronger than the soul and continually thwarts the reality of God's indwelling love and holiness that is known to the soul. However, on the soul journey, the soul grows in strength and maturity and is able, with practice, to convert the ego into thoughts of positive love. As ego is converted into love, our beings are happier and more content; they become peaceful and joyful within themselves, and grow in love and respect for others Our beings begin to know God in reality—a God who desires only our good and loves us wholeheartedly.

Ego learned to act negatively toward others from the beginning of our lives, in order that it might feel superior to others. Yet ego is confused because, in its insecurity, it is also negative towards itself continually putting itself down and declaring itself unworthy of love. In order for ego to be converted, it needs to be loved by the spirit and soul; it needs to be drawn into our whole being, and know itself as a respected member, not only of the individual being, but also of the whole of mankind.

The conversion of ego is accomplished with patient practice. Every time the ego shouts or whispers that you are no good, the soul will gently refute the accusation with a positive response of your goodness and holiness. When ego tells you that others are no good or are against you, your soul voice will be strong in declaring that this is not so, and that they are loving, in need of your kindness, and of God's holy love. If ego tells you that God is out to get you, has made you sick because you are bad, or does not love you, spirit and soul will gather strength together and, with quiet power, declare that God loves you and has only your good in mind.

Ego can be converted to join with your soul and spirit to say love is the answer—love of God, love of others, and love of yourself.

GOD AT THE CENTER

There was a time in Christianity when every part of the day was anchored in God from morning's rising to night time's lying down to rest. I think we can reclaim this way of life. It is not too far fetched to think that we could claim our lives for the Blessed Trinity; to be aware that we are surrounded and indwelt by the Triune God.

Looking back on such a time, it seems almost charming and whimsical that every part of the day could be an occasion for a blessing. The woman who wove her cloth asked a blessing on the loom and each of its parts; the man who farmed the field asked a blessing on the planting of the seeds and a good harvest for his crops. Is there any reason why we cannot do the same for the modern-day tools of our work—our washing machines, our computers, and our gardens, to name a few?

Because in modern-day Christianity we tend to keep God on the outskirts of our lives—placing God on a special day of the week or asking a blessing on a meal only when we have a guest—the Sacred One is kept at arm's length and in the place we have designated for God. Instead of keeping God at the periphery of our world we can bring God to the center of our lives. Having God at our center makes the Sacred One pivotal in all we do.

If we become sick, have an accident, or a special concern we bring the Holy One out of the God-box and demand special favors and answers to our needs. It is embarrassing that we use God in this way. If God were always the central focus of our lives, we could be forgiven for asking special favors at difficult times; but if God were the central focus of our lives, then it would not be a case of asking for *special* favors but focusing our trust on God in extraordinary times as we do in all our times—good and bad. It becomes another way to entrust our lives to God.

To the early Celtic Christian, times of dark and light were part of the rhythm of life; in times of sickness and health, poverty and wealth, or fasting and feasting, God was trusted, thanked, and praised as the central reason for being.

In the beginning of Celtic Christianity we see God at the center of people's lives. God was brought into every thing that was done, from getting out of bed in the morning to laying down again at night; from lighting the fire in the morning to tamping down the fire at the end of the day; from the baby's birth and his dedication to God at the first breath of life, through the daily living of that life, to the last moment of life with the return of the body to the earth and the spirit to heaven.

The lay Celtic Christians were, in essence, contemplatives without a cloister. They lived and worked their lives with an undercurrent of prayer. They lived close to God always; they lived as a community with their neighbors; and they lived close to nature. They lived a life of wholeness; there was no separation of prayer from work or work from prayer. They lived lives totally aware of God's presence in all that they did and said; they lived lives in partnership with God.

Though I consider myself as a contemplative without a cloister, I know that I have not reached the level of spiritual living that these early Celtic Christians lived. I need to be reminded each time I do something to do it in the name of God, in prayer to God, and in reverence for the task at hand along with its tools.

Making meals, feeding the animals, cleaning the litter boxes, doing the laundry, baking bread, driving to work, riding public transportation, doing grocery shopping, entering our places of work, returning home, using the computer, exercising, and any other things we do should all be occasions for uniting our lives with God, giving God praise and thanksgiving, and asking a blessing on all our activities.

Until we remember to make our lives wholly one with God; until we remember that God is the very center of our lives; until we remember to do all in the name of the Trinity, it is a good idea to write some prayers for every task we perform, print them on cards, and place them where our eyes can see them as we perform our work. Eventually, they will become part of our spiritual lifestyle, the undercurrent of prayer that holds us in God's hands at all times, blessing our lives in the name of Jesus Christ.

Prayers throughout the day are becoming more of a natural thing for me; prayer, as undercurrent of my life in all I do, upholds me and keeps me ever mindful of God's presence with me, in me, and around me. Ceaseless praise and prayer, blessing and thanksgiving, intercession and supplication, should be my delight and joy and is becoming so; the more I am aware of God in every part of my life and practice, I find myself speaking to the Lord as I go from one task to another.

Holiness sings out its joy in words of love and praise, ever mindful of the Holy Trinity living within me; ever mindful of the Holy Trinity surrounding me with protection and love; ever mindful of the Holy Trinity walking before me to guide me on the path and behind me to protect me from all ill; ever mindful of the Holy Trinity walking beside me as companion along my way. Each member of the Trinity is with me—the Father who created me and goes on creating me each day; Jesus, the Son, my Savior and Shepherd, leading me through good pastures each new day; and the Holy Spirit who blesses me in everything I do, moving across the spiritual waters to give new life. I praise God, I bless God, and I give thanks to God, Father, Son, and Holy Spirit; Holy Trinity, Triune God.

MODERN DAY PRAYERS IN THE CELTIC MANNER

The following poems are a few examples of prayers I have composed in the Celtic manner to use as I go about my various chores.

Pilgrimage Process

Baking Bread

This bread I bake, O Lord,
Is not the bread for Eucharist.
It is the bread for family—
For husband, child and me.
As you, O Lord, blessed loaves and fishes
And multiplied them for the crowd,
Bless now, this bread that I am baking
And bless us all who share this loaf.

Bless the Tools of my Work

Bless, O Father, my creative work this day;
Bless, O Son, the writing;
Bless with energy, O Holy Spirit,
The work to be done this day.
I ask a blessing upon the power of electricity,
The power that enables my computer to work.
Bless, O Lord, the source of this power,
The rushing stream, the power plant,
The person who controls the flow of water over the dam.
Bless, O Lord, the source.
Bless, O Lord, the power plant,
Every cog and wheel;
Each person who co-ordinates the power supply
To our homes, our streets, our factories.
Bless, O Lord, the power plant.
Bless, O Lord, the hydro workers,
Each one who works on power lines;
Protect them from shocks and burnings,
From high voltage and falling lines.
Bless, O Lord, and keep them safe
As they maintain and repair these lines.
Bless, O Lord, the hydro workers.
Bless, O Lord, this computer, where I work this day;
Protect it from mischief,
From power surges and viruses;
Bless the hard drive, the software,

HIGHWAY OF HOLINESS

The keyboard and the printer;
Protect my work from being lost.
Bless, O Lord, this computer.
Bless the work that comes from you,
Through my mind and heart and hands;
Bless the pen, computer and printer,
That put the work on paper;
Bless and protect the work, O Lord.

The Journey

Bless to me, O God,
The earth beneath my feet;
Bless to me, O God,
The path whereon I walk;
Bless to me, O God,
The road beneath my car;
Bless to me, O God,
The street whereon I drive.
Bless to me, O God,
The steering wheel within my hands;
Bless to me, O God,
The way wherein I'm led.
Bless to me, O God,
The road that takes me out;
Bless to me, O God,
The path that leads back home.

DEPTH AND UNIQUENESS
OF OUR RELATIONSHIP WITH GOD

I am beginning to understand the depth of my relationship with God, and that I have a unique relationship with the Sacred. John O'Donahue explains it this way, "The deeper ground of individuality is to be sought in the originality of the Divine Imagination manifest in the relish of beginnings. The Divine Artist is utterly creative, makes each thing new and different. Each individual expresses and incarnates a different dimension of divinity. Each one of us comes from a different place in the circle of the Divine. Consequently each one of us prays out of a different inner world and each one of us prays to a different place in the Divine Circle."[2]

This gives me a totally unique way of praying; a special expression of prayer from my life, my essence, and my being; a prayer that has a direct line to God's heart. Each one of us has a different door into God's divinity; each one of us stands on our individual threshold where we join with God in our God-given way and direction.

As we grow in spiritual maturity, we learn to trust the uniqueness of our own soul; we see the beauty that God has bestowed upon our soul; we hear the voice and melody in our soul, combining it with the rhythm of our heart and the depth of our prayer beat.

To join in saying the prayers of the church is good, especially when we are in a church service for it brings unity and community to the congregation. It is equally good to pray the deep individual prayer of our soul and heart that reaches into the divine heart of the Creator. This prayer sometimes is beyond words; it is total essence of divine love; it is a yearning, longing, and deep desire to be one with God; to be fully ourselves and fully divine; to be holy because God is holy; to feel the sacredness of our created being, of our soul's center, and of our heart's beat.

We are poised on the glorious unique threshold of the open door between God and our being; between the Creator and the created. You are totally unique; I am totally unique. The Creator made each one of us in God's holiness, from God's sacredness, and in God's joyous creativity. As such, we each pray to God in a completely one-of-a-kind way, and long to be at one with the Sacred One and grow in God's spirit of holiness.

We are born in holiness; our essence is holiness; holiness is the core of our being. It is the eternal soul that is holy; before we

---

2. O'Donahue, *Eternal Echoes*, 207.

became physical beings and after we cease to be physical beings, our soul is eternal essence and its eternal essence is holiness.

This soul, this essential part of us, is not tangible. The soul does not have a specific position in our bodies as do our physical organs such as the liver or the heart. At times, I envision the soul as a vibrant, pulsating light; like a mandala or a sphere with ever-changing colors. I think of the soul as pervading every part of my being with its essence; and I think of my soul as encompassing me, enfolding me in its completeness, and surrounding me as with an aura of holy light. This essential part of us, our soul, is holy and seeks constantly to transform our whole being—body, intellect, emotion, and ego—into complete holiness.

I was created in holiness; you were created in holiness. I am holy; you are holy; and we are each walking the spiritual Highway of Holiness, and our soul is making the journey and showing us the way.

3

Starting Our Spiritual Journey

THE STARTING point of our spiritual pilgrimage is different for each one of us and develops differently according to our family circumstances as well as our physical, intellectual, and emotional make up. To give you an example, I will share a little of the beginnings of my life.

When I was a child, no more than six years old, we got our milk fresh from a local farm. At that time, I lived in South Wales in sight of the Brecon Beacons and I enjoyed a healthy life in a country setting, breathing in the fresh outdoor air. All was as perfect as it could be for a child of those times and my parents must have been devastated when they discovered that the good life they struggled to give me—including fresh produce from the farm—was the very thing that caused me to become sick at such a young age.

I developed bovine tuberculosis (T.B.) from drinking fresh milk from the farm, from cows that had not been tested for T.B. and whose milk had not been pasteurized. Why the rest of the family didn't get it I don't know, but so began one of the earliest stages in my life on the Highway of Holiness.

I did not take the beginnings of my journey well. I was a fighter; I was a screamer, and I screamed in particular at the daily treatments of hot poultices needed to cure my disease. And yet, I learned that I had to go through what came, no matter how much I screamed against it. Even then, God was preparing me, and my soul was leading me, in a life that would mature spiritually day by day.

My nature was one of rebellion against outside forces, mixed in with a great desire to be spiritually tranquil. I longed to be good and holy yet my temper flew out at anything that went against me and my will. My soul was guiding my being to let go of fear, so as to become pure and holy, an instrument for God's love in this world.

My screaming self needed guidance in its growth to become spiritually mature, and my soul took on that task. My journey on the Highway of Holiness has been long and has been protected every step of the way by God. My journey is far from over yet. My desire is to be tranquil, contemplative, given wholly to God, and to serve the Sacred One in whatever way I am asked.

THE LORD'S CALL

I feel the Lord's call to me is to pray and to write; God calls me to search more deeply so as to come to know the intimate part of my being—the soul part of me—and to go even further in depth in order to know God—the ground of my being—without whom I would not even be here on this earth and in this life.

We desire to know God's searching and God's longing for us; we become one with God's searching and one with God's longing, so that we become one being with God in the circle of the Trinity. The undercurrent of divine love and life flows through us. That undercurrent is the Holy Spirit, the constant life-giving force that supports the holy life that we have been given.

The soul calls out for God; the soul desires to be in the circle of God's holiness; the soul that is a very part of God transforms the rest of our being into holiness. Prayer is the staying-power that enables us to always be at one with God—God-focused; one-souled with God; one-hearted with God; one-minded with God. As God desires to be with us, at one with us, so we would be at one with God.

God's holiness calls us; our holiness responds with joy. We do not understand this bond; but what is there to understand? God created us and formed each one of us—the core of the holy beings we are becoming. Before we were born, we made a contract with the Sacred One that we would grow into the special persons we are each becoming. Renew your commitment now to grow and mature in spiritual evolution as an individual and as part of the spiritual community to which you belong.

As the caterpillar must wrap itself in its silken cocoon in order to become a butterfly, so we must enter into the depth of our soul to learn the Holy Spirit's sacred secrets in order that we may be clothed in holiness and become transformed into spiritual beings.

NO SEPARATION BETWEEN SECULAR AND SACRED

You enter into the depth of your being into the soul presence, into the prayer presence, where you are one with the Sacred; where you are one with yourself; where you and God are one being. The soul holds you together in its home; in the core of your being where God and you are one, one essence, and one holy reality.

There is no separation between sacred and secular. God is the Creator of all life; your human self, created in the Circle of God and planted in your mother's womb, may have forgotten its holy beginnings, but the soul draws you into its memory where you can recover the sense of holiness that was given in God's creation of you. Holiness is God's being and you are holy because God is holy and God created you. Receive this gift of holiness and hold it in your hands.

When I first observed the gift, I looked at it with reverence and wonder, and marveled that I had not recognized it sooner. Holiness is a part of me that I did not recognize until late in life. The soul has kept this holiness intact and safe from warring passions within and without me. The soul is the repository of this holy gift, this sacred essence; the soul has shared it with me as I have been able to understand it and accept it. The soul has made me aware of the precious holy essence of God and I receive it with thanks and awe.

It is through the daily spiritual pilgrimage, the daily walk on the Highway of Holiness that we become mature enough to receive the holiness that has always been a part of us. If only we had seen this holiness sooner, how much healing of the world could have taken place? Observing children and their desire to help those in need, I have come to understand that those who are young use their inner holiness naturally and without second guessing themselves. They have not lost the state of holiness that was with them from birth—it is lost along the way of life through the influence of outside forces.

The holiness we had at birth becomes lost and forgotten as we are battered and bruised by unseen forces of evil along our path. That is why the soul is designated to keep it safe until such time as we are able to take it back and integrate holiness into our whole being. When we become one with the Sacred, and are strong enough in prayer to once again wear holiness as a complete garment, then the soul allows holiness to shine forth and we are clothed completely, within and without, in holy raiment.

We are whole at last, body, mind, and spirit, completely at one with God. We have brought our joys and sorrows, our sicknesses and health, our difficulties and happiness into our soul's prayer life and they have all been blended together with our holy essence until we become at home with our holy selves. We are at peace; tranquil and serene; we are whole and holy.

It is the patient work of our faithful souls that brings us to this point where we are a part of the circle of God's Being—a living, holy part of God—and God is at home in the core of our being. Our life becomes whole, complete, and sacred; balanced, quiet, and gentle. The fruit of the Spirit ripens and becomes mature; the harvest of the Spirit comes to maturity, is faithfully gathered by the soul, and is stored in the soul. Its essence can now be set free to heal the wounds of the world.

SOUL POTENTIAL

The spiritual journey to maturity involves the development of the soul's potential and the fruit of the Spirit. The soul's resources are innate in us at birth, at least in seed form, but they develop, grow, and strengthen by being put to use as our beings grow into wholeness. As muscles of the body gain strength by exercise, so the soul's qualities grow the more they are put into practice. The more we listen to and become attuned to the soul's voice, the stronger it becomes and the more easily we are able to recognize it. At the same time, the soul's language becomes clearer and we are more easily able to understand it.

The fruits of the spirit mentioned in St. Paul's letter to the Galatians (5:22) are some of the characteristics (maybe only in seed form as yet) found in the soul and being brought to maturity. The list that St. Paul gives: love, joy, peace, patience, kindness, goodness, faithfulness, gentleness, and self-control, are not meant to be exhaustive but, if pursued and developed by the Spirit, will take us a good distance along the pilgrim path.

In his letter to the Colossians (3:12, 15), Paul speaks of tenderhearted mercy, kindness, humility, gentleness, patience, and peace; in Ephesians (4:2), of humility and gentleness; in his first letter to Timothy (6:11), of faith, love, perseverance, and gentleness.

James, in his letter says, "The wisdom from above is first of all pure. It is also peace loving, gentle at all times, and willing to yield to others. It is full of mercy and good deeds" (Jas 3:17a).

Carolyn Myss says, "You uncover the different qualities of power that each soul contains, all of which the individual needs to explore and refine, including humility, dignity, integrity, honor, wisdom, justice, harmony, and endurance."[1]

If we make a list, then, of the fruits of the spirit or soul qualities named by Paul, James, and Myss, we would have the following: love, joy, peace, kindness, goodness, faithfulness, gentleness,

---

1. Myss, *Entering The Castle*, 57.

self-control, humility, dignity, integrity, honor, wisdom, justice, harmony, endurance, perseverance, mercy, and purity; and when we look at this list we note that they are qualities that are quiet and unobtrusive. The soul's strength is in its calmness and serenity, its tranquility and discretion; it draws others to itself by its restrained and restful manner and not in showy, busy, or noisy behavior.

The soul's qualities or spiritual fruits reside in, and emerge from, deep within the core of one's being, and as the seeds within the soul mature into spiritual fruits, one's whole being shows even deeper quietness and peaceful dignity.

The mature spiritual fruit is not flamboyant or audacious, enticing others to garishness or frivolity; it draws others to live in peace and harmony, quiet joy, happiness, and belonging. Others feel at home in the gardens of our souls and spirits; they are glad to rest and find spiritual renewal there.

As the soul seeds develop, other travelers will find the banks and hedgerows along our spiritual highway to be a delight to the eyes and rest to the soul.

SILENCE AND PRAYER

As nourishment for the body builds up physical strength; as reading and study build up mental acuity; so silence and prayer expand the soul. Grace and wisdom received from God during our prayer times are kept safe within the soul by the practice of silence. Silence guards God's grace and wisdom within our souls; silence is the milieu in which the gifts of the Spirit grow and expand; and silence is the essence through which God's gifts of grace and wisdom are disseminated to others.

I do not mean that we are to keep silence as one would in a monastery or convent where the monks and nuns keep silence at certain hours and in specific places, where the rule does not allow talking with one another except at times of recreation, so that an environment of prayer may pervade the building. I mean that we shouldn't chatter carelessly with anyone we meet about messages or guidance we receive from God in our prayer times—this can lead to boasting or competition, which will stunt the growth of our souls. Silence is the soul's venue of expansion and growth.

There will be very few people and very few times when specific instances of God's leading will be shared with others. Those who are given to us by God as our soul companions or our spiritual directors should be the only ones with whom we will share God's guidance. The silence of the soul will be its own way of allowing God's gifts of grace to be shared with others.

As when seeds are planted in the ground they are covered with earth to allow them to put down deep roots in the darkness and only then to sprout shoots into the surrounding air and light, so the seeds of God's grace are kept in the silence of our souls to allow their roots to grow strong and deep. Then it is that God's grace and wisdom begin to sprout and can be seen by others with no need of spoken explanation.

CONTEMPLATIVES WITHOUT CLOISTERS

We want to be contemplatives without cloisters; we desire to be one with the divine without leaving the world, without separating ourselves from the ordinary. Is this possible? If we are willing to pursue the call, yes, I believe it is possible.

The call is to pray, to be at one with the Sacred at any and every given moment. Answering the call to prayer allows us to become aware of the strong support given to the whole world through this continual flow to God in the never ending undercurrent of prayer. Communion with God throughout our days and nights sees God's leading in each and every moment whether the moment is revealed in dark's difficulties or light's joy; and always we see it revealed in God's love.

This call to be a contemplative without a cloister can only be answered in faith believing that the Holy Spirit will continue

HIGHWAY OF HOLINESS

to lead us along the Highway of Holiness and enable us to grow in spiritual maturity whether the way is difficult or easy. We will encounter in life our share of hard times and our portion of easy times but, whether hard or easy, all times are God's times—our times with God.

God calls us to his purpose and we call on God to ask for more details as to why we were born; we ask to what spiritual path we have been called; we ask if there will be guidance on our way. God says, "Here I am; I am closer to you than your own breath; we walk this path together; spiritual mysteries that will astonish you are opened before you as you walk your spiritual journey, your Highway of Holiness."

GOD'S MIRACLES IN THE EVERYDAY

At the end of 2006 I was getting very discouraged about getting my latest book of meditations published. My manuscript, Glorious Autumn Days, had just been turned down by a third publisher. This was to be expected. I knew it would eventually be accepted by someone but I didn't want to wait. I wanted this book out in the hands of the public sooner than some mythical time in the future. I was looking for a miracle from God, a *specific* miracle; I was looking for a publisher to come and sweep my book to immediate publication.

In my journal, on December 6th, 2006, I noted that I had read in Brendan Doyle's book about Julian of Norwich the following words written by Julian:

> "God does not want
> us to be burdened
> because of sorrows and tempests
> that happen in our lives,
> because
> it has always been so
> before miracles happen."[2]

2. Doyle, *Meditations With Julian of Norwich*, 63.

Following these words, I said, "I pray that a miracle will now happen. I will not be burdened by my sorrow, knowing that this is the way it is before a miracle. I, therefore, Lord, await my miracle."

A few days later, I realized that God had anticipated my need for a miracle and I had already received my miracle in advance of knowing that I needed it but I had not recognized it. The week before I had been rejected by the third publisher, I had been given the name of a self-publishing website; the name came to me out of the blue through a third party. But, at that time, my mind was closed to it—I had always said that I would never go the self-publishing route—well, never say never! Once I realized that this leading was of God I ran with it. I have published three books on the internet since that time and was satisfied with the results for that particular time in my writing life.

God does not always work in specifics. God often works in surprises and we have to be open to the answer that comes to us unexpectedly and not be afraid to accept the gift. I was expecting God to miraculously send me a publisher but God made me aware of self-publishing as a viable option. It was up to me to recognize my miracle and receive it. I self-published Glorious Autumn Days, despite little computer savvy and, in 2007 my book and my own website were launched with success.

CHANGE YOUR RESPONSE FROM FEAR TO LOVE

We are often afraid to open ourselves to God's miracles because of fear of the unknown or because we are afraid of what God will expect from us in return. Why should we be afraid? God only wants our good. We need to change our response from fear to love and the only way to do this is through practice.

Your response of fear may have its roots deep in your past. Perhaps you were sick as a child and had to undergo painful and unpleasant tests and treatments. Perhaps they made you afraid because you didn't understand what was happening to you. Now, if you become ill, your first response is one of fear and maybe even panic. You anticipate pain, anxiety, and abandonment. How can you possibly turn this around into something positive?

You may wonder what manner of love there could be in such a stressful time as illness. You may wonder why God would allow you to go through illness in the first place. How, you may wonder, could God be a God of love if he allows you to suffer?

Illness and suffering are a part of life on earth. Fear is a response to this part of life and fear makes the suffering more unbearable—it exacerbates it. If you change your response from fear of the illness and fear of pain toward receiving God's love; if you turn from dwelling on your fear toward seeking the love that surrounds you—God's love or a friend's love—your fear will lessen. You have to practice over and over to change your response from fear to love. Every time you respond in fear to a particular circumstance, you have to consciously stop in your thought-tracks and turn your response to one of love. Look toward God's love; be aware of the God of love dwelling within you; be aware that you are abiding in the God of love. It is the soul that shows you the way. Listen to the voice of your soul.

St. John tells us in his first letter, "God is love, and all who live in love live in God, and God lives in them . . . Such love has no fear, because perfect love expels all fear. If we are afraid, it is for fear of punishment, and this shows that we have not fully experienced his perfect love" (1 John 4:16b, 18).

We may want to experience this perfect love but it is difficult for many of us to change from a fear response to a love response because we are actually afraid to love—we are afraid to give love and we are afraid to receive love. We may have been discouraged from showing love as we grew up; we may have shown love to someone and that love may have been rejected. If demonstrations of love are discouraged often enough, we will stop showing our love to others and discourage others from showing love to us for fear of being reprimanded or ridiculed.

In order to heal the world and bring God's perfect love into the world, we have to first heal ourselves of our fear of love and acknowledge the presence of God's perfect love dwelling in us. This is a very important step on our soul journey, not only for our own growth in spiritual maturity but also in the world's spiritual growth. We have to enlist the soul to teach us how to discard fear and how to love.

Each time you are aware of a fear thought, immediately think a love thought. Each time you are aware of a negative thought about another person or situation, replace it with a positive thought. You need to turn on the light of God's love, shine it onto the negative habits and turn them into positive habits. Turn fear into love, hate into love, criticism into love, and jealousy into love. This is how miracles happen in the world—they happen first in you; this is how the world is healed—you heal yourself first.

BREAKING THE CYCLE

When we fall back into old habits and old fears, the devil thinks that he has us in his grasp. In times when we revert to our old ways the devil may well get a hold of us, not because we sinned but because the sinful act or bad habit makes us afraid to return to God. We may feel that we have let God down; we may feel frustrated because we thought we had come so far along the road to God and, for one moment's pleasure or rebellion, we turned our backs on the Lord; for one moment of fear, we forgot God's love; for one step into a negative habit, we took a step into the darkness.

It is not this one act that takes us from God's holiness and the holy calling of joy, but our continual playing of the refrain, "I am not worthy". We have to break that cycle as soon as we are aware of what we are doing. The enemy's triumph is in his grasping our one bad habit or our one fearful act and using it as an opportunity to get our attention away from God. We must turn our backs on the devil, turn deaf ears to his voice, and turn our hearts to God.

Ask for God's forgiveness; do not hesitate to tell the Sacred One that you're back with God where you belong, that you don't want to be apart from the Lord for one moment. God will forgive you, love you, and celebrate your return to the Lord. Rejoice! All God wants is your good. Christ's parable of the Prodigal Son (Luke 15:11–32) shows this very well.

Begin a prayer of thanksgiving, love, joy and gentleness. Stop denigrating yourself. Each time you return to God after you have turned away from the Lord, and each time you return more quickly to God, shows your greater desire for good than evil.

> Then Jesus said, "Come to me, all of you who are weary and carry heavy burdens, and I will give you rest. Take my yoke upon you. Let me teach you, because I am humble and gentle at heart, and you will find rest for your souls." (Matt 11:28–29)

GOD DOES NOT ABANDON US

> My heart is breaking as I remember how it used to be: I walked among the crowd of worshipers, leading a great procession to the house of God, singing for joy and giving thanks amid the sound of a great celebration! Why am I discouraged? Why is my heart so sad? I will put my hope in God! I will praise him again—my Savior and my God! (Ps 42:4–6a)

> But each day the Lord pours his unfailing love upon me, and through each night I sing his songs, praying to God who gives me life. (Ps 42:8)

Writers know all about good times and bad. Some articles are accepted while others are rejected. Words flow easily on the page one day but the next there are no words to be found to express the idea one has in one's mind.

For a few weeks, when my writing was going very well, I found my life to be good and peaceful. During this time I was very upbeat. "How good God is to me," I said, "see how God helps me with my writing." I gave praise and thanks to God. Then the words and ideas dried up and I felt betrayed.

I wondered why God's goodness had been withdrawn from me. I became discouraged because of God's apparent abandonment. I began to reason it out in my prayer journal. Why had I become down-hearted? If God gave me help when things were going well, how much more would God assist me when things were not going well?

Whether things are going well or not, God is with us; God doesn't forsake us. God doesn't abandon us because we make a mistake; rather God assists us to pick up the pieces and start over.

If we get sick it is not a punishment for wrongdoing. Even if we have done something wrong God does not punish us by making us ill. Whether we are sick or well God is with us. We are not sick because we are bad; just the same as we are not well because we are good. We are sick or well because that's the way it is and no matter what, God will be with us; God will not abandon us.

We, too, must try not to abandon God. When things are going well we should celebrate with the Lord and when things are going badly we should talk to the Sacred One. God will console us and strengthen us so that we can get through this difficult time.

> Why am I discouraged? Why is my heart so sad? (Ps 42:11a)

Why indeed? Just yesterday I was full of joy, I was ready to praise the Lord and give thanks for God's goodness to me. God's goodness to me hasn't changed. I may have concerns about my health or my writing, but that doesn't mean God has abandoned me. This is all the more reason for God to be with me and for me to hold on fast to God.

As we go along the journey of life we will have some rough patches and some smooth passages. The spiritual journey is woven into the journey of life. Along life's road, all parts of our being are growing and maturing—our minds gain more knowledge, our bodies grow stronger as we exercise them, and our souls gradually become filled with grace. In all the growing that we do, spiritual growth may be the least recognized—the spirit is not measured in exam or contest results and, therefore, we are often not aware of the presence of the spirit let alone the importance of its growth as we go through life.

It is often when we go through difficult times that we become aware of the spiritual side of our being. We become aware of our need of a Higher Power to get us through the rough spots and a Supreme Being to whom we can give thanks when we do get through these times safely and with new understanding.

> I will put my hope in God! I will praise him again—my Savior and my God! (Ps 42:11b)

God helps me to keep a happy face, a sparkle in my eyes; my countenance reflects God's help and presence with me. I will be serene and composed, no matter what comes. God gives me support, and is present with me whether I understand what's happening or not. God is there quietly with me as an earthly friend stands by me and gives me support in a crisis.

Our reward is being with God and God living in us.

WE NEED GOD'S SPECIAL PROTECTION IN GOOD TIMES

All areas of life's journey are subject to periods of long, slow, and imperceptible change, alternating with periods of quick, sudden spurts of growth. Sometimes, after little change in a child's height over a long period of time he may suddenly gain several inches very quickly; associated with this the child may suffer from joint pains or muscle cramps and may be told that he is experiencing growing pains. Some young people may have difficulty in reading and writing, while others have trouble understanding math;

Starting Our Spiritual Journey

then, suddenly, these areas may become clear to them—everything seems to fall into place.

As you go on your spiritual pilgrimage you will probably find that much of your journey is without difficulty; you may not have any spiritual highs or lows, you may just keep plodding along. During these times you may get complacent; you may lose your vigilance; you may get bored with putting one foot in front of the other on your everyday walk; you may begin to take these uneventful times for granted and even think that it is your right to have an easy go of it.

When things go well for us on the soul journey we need special protection, a special guard to keep us safe. We need a special gift from God, to keep us walking humbly and joyfully in the Lord's sight. It is easy to get puffed up with pride and rush on ahead when our projects do well. But this is the very time we must walk in step with God, side by side with Christ.

There's nothing wrong with being excited when we are getting ahead in life, but it is easy in our excitement to forget the root and anchor of our lives. We must continue to walk humbly with God.

The word "humble" when used to describe ourselves is a scary word. If we say that we are humble, isn't that pride? How can we describe ourselves as humble? What gives us the right to think that we are humble? If we were really humble, we probably wouldn't be aware of it, because we would be too humble to recognize it.

However, we can recognize if we are getting ahead of ourselves and ahead of God by thinking that we are so great now that we don't need God's support anymore. The only reason that we don't need to seek God's support is that we already have it. If we don't have the Lord's support or if we have deliberately abandoned it, we will very soon be aware of our need of it—we won't be able to function without it.

We need to ask God to hold us in the training reins—we need to stay yoked with him—as we walk forward on our soul journey. If we pull ahead of God it will cause chafing and disruption. We must walk step by step, day by day, path by path, and prayer by prayer with God, listening all the while to God's guidance. The soul will issue warnings; we need to listen to the soul's voice within us and follow the soul's leading. We do not necessarily hear actual words; there may be a feeling or an instinct of what we should do. The more we are attuned to the voice that the soul uses to communicate with us, the more quickly we will respond to what the soul tells us.

WALKING THE FUTURE IN SAFETY

> The Lord had said to Abram, "Leave your native country, your relatives, and your father's family, and go to the land that I will show you." . . . So Abram departed as the Lord had instructed, and Lot went with him. (Gen 12:1, 4a)

Would you be willing to follow the Lord's path as quickly as Abram did? If the Lord called you to go somewhere else, would you do it? It would not be an easy decision, but if God asks you to go somewhere else or do something else, help will be provided. You would not be alone. Abram did as the Lord said and Lot went with him.

When I was in my early twenties and living in England, I, along with some fellow Registered Nurses, decided to go to Canada. We planned to work in Canada for a year with a view to emigrating there permanently. As the time grew close, my would-be companions backed out of the adventure. I did not hesitate for a moment. I knew that I was meant to go to Canada and, though I was now alone, I went through with my decision. As I look back on my life from where I am now, in my seventies, I see God's hand in that decision and all that has happened to me since.

I did not think of it then as God's will for me; but now, more than fifty years since that decision, I know with certainty that it was God's guidance and direction that I should come to Canada. I sometimes wonder what my life would have been like if I had not followed God's leading on this path. I *did* listen to God's direction and I *did* follow where God led. I am still led along the spiritual path for me and I give thanks for God's faithfulness.

We ask the Lord to show us God's way and we ask that God will stay with us along the path. We need to recover a sense of safety and faith in God's call. We may have fear of going forward, taking the next step, or starting again, but we must proceed knowing that the Lord will watch over our going out and our coming in. We must ask God to assist us to keep going through difficult terrain, help us to walk in safety, and not be afraid. The soul that lives in the core of our being; the soul that is God's home, will provide the strength we need to overcome our fears, if we listen to her voice.

> I was glad when they said to me, "Let us go to the house of the Lord." And now here we are, standing inside your gates, O Jerusalem. (Ps 122:1–2)

We ask God to make it a blessing that we are a part of the house of prayer. God is here with us, we are here with God, and that's all that matters. Together, we can do wonders; together we make the clouds disappear; together we hold the world in mercy, love, and joy. As contemplatives living outside a cloister and as prayer warriors living within the world, we are part of the house of prayer.

This morning, as I write in my journal, the sky is full of clouds and rain that speak a message of doom. Thoughts lie heavily upon me that we might have a storm so severe that all could soon be destroyed. But I cannot live in thoughts of what might happen. The present moment and how I handle it is the only important thing, for this moment is all I really have. All my prayers of love and joy are gathered in this moment, to be borne hence to God and from God to the place where they are needed.

Together with God, we can do anything. Of course, God can do anything without us, but God gives us the opportunity to share in the healing of the world, in mercy, love, and joy. God's gifts are dispersed into the world through our prayers, and we receive God's gifts into our lives through the prayers of others. We are all part of the one body, the one Christ, and the one house of the Lord. When we work together, a glorious mandala appears—a mandala of colors, prayers, and paths within the house of God, the world's soul.

The soul's voice within each one of us and within the community of God becomes stronger as we listen for that voice and begin to recognize it. Practice listening and becoming attuned to the gentle insistence of the voice of your soul.

4

Meeting Others on the Journey

PEOPLE ARE GIFTS FROM GOD

It is important to consider all those with whom we come in contact on our journey as gifts from God. It is not just those whom we love and who love us that are God's emissaries but also those whom we don't find easy to tolerate; they too are given to us by God for some purpose. There is a divine reason for each person with whom we meet on our journey.

When we meet up with someone on our soul journey, it is because we have been brought together through God's ordinance and purpose. This purpose may not be shown to us until some later point in our lives. What a cause of thanksgiving and joy this is to us when God's purpose for this meeting on our journey is made known. Such a revelation in our lives brings us to a realization and recognition that God guides us through our whole lives from birth to death, leading us each step of the way.

If we look back over our lives, the map laid out for our spiritual pilgrimage is clear—this map has been and continues to be in God's beholding from the beginning of creation to our present day lives and beyond into the future of mankind. God has the end point of our journey fully perfected in divine sight from the beginning. God has multiple roads with alternate routes that lead each one of us to God's ultimate destiny for us, and this destiny is abundant life in the Sacred One.

The moment by moment journey on the spiritual Highway of Holiness is all-important as we pursue our daily path. There will be times of difficulty on the journey, times when we will become discouraged. At such times as these, it is a good exercise to look back over our journey to see and acknowledge God's working in our lives.

Take the time to reproduce God's map of your particular spiritual journey. Using ten year increments, write down as many minor, major, ordinary, and extraordinary events as you can recall in your life, and look at how they brought you to this moment where you are now on your growth to spiritual maturity and your relationship with God.

As you look back, do you see major or urgent points of moving on or changing direction? Do you see times where you rested along the way, allowing your spiritual seed to put down deep roots and push up tender shoots, a period of quiet strengthening before proceeding on the soul journey?

What does God's spiritual road map of your life look like from the beginning until now? Can you begin to see God's design in your life so far? Does this give you confidence in God's plan for your continued growth toward oneness with the Sacred One? Do you see an inkling of God's purpose in those people whom you met along the way?

STORIES OF PEOPLE WHO MET IN THE BIBLE

In the Old Testament, we read about a time of famine during the life of Elijah, the prophet. Elijah is hungry and comes upon a widow who is about to use the last of her supplies to make a meal for herself and her son. This meeting between Elijah and the widow was just like any meeting we might have on our journey today.

> Elijah said to [the widow], "Don't be afraid! Go ahead and do just what you've said, but make a little bread for me first. Then use what's left to prepare a meal for yourself and your son. For this is what the Lord, the God of Israel, says: There will always be flour and olive oil left in your containers until the time when the Lord sends rain and the crops grow again!" (1 Kgs 17:13–14)

The widow had only enough oil and barley to make one last meal for her and her son; this is what she had planned to do and then they were going to lie down and die. The prophet Elijah asked her to make him some bread first before she tended to herself and her son. She hesitated because reason told her that if she did that, she would have nothing left for herself. But Elijah, in the name of God, told her that if she did what he asked then she and her son would have enough to last until the drought was over. He told her that the container of oil would not run dry and the barrel of flour would not run out.

The widow used the last of her provisions to feed Elijah as he asked. Even though she thought that she and her son would now die of starvation, she sensed that this man was a man of God and perhaps she thought that they would die a good death and be rewarded in heaven for their service to a holy man. The widow was in fact rewarded on earth; all three of them had enough to eat for the duration of the drought as God had promised through the word of Elijah. The container of oil and the barrel of flour were never empty because she had acted on what the prophet had told her. Perhaps she didn't really believe, but she did it anyway.

She might have said, "If you are a prophet why doesn't God give the oil and flour directly to you, so that you can make your own bread?" But God often works through us, and allows the divine to be dependent on us to fulfill God's works and deeds of love. That way our hearts grow in love so that we can give and receive in God's name.

You may have seen this in your own life. Your instincts say, "Do this," but your practical side says that you can't afford it. Your instincts tell you that if you follow your heart you will be rewarded and your creativity will be renewed. Maybe you don't really believe what your instincts tell you but you act anyway, hoping that it might be true though expecting that you will be disappointed or rejected. How surprised and delighted you are when you are rewarded for following your instincts. How your heart expands and opens in trust to God.

Of course, immediate rewards may not be seen even when we do something spectacular such as the widow did when using all her supplies to feed Elijah. We are not doing good deeds in order to get rewarded. As Jesus says, "If someone demands your coat, offer your shirt also. Give to anyone who asks; and when things are taken away from you, don't try to get them back" Luke 6:29b–30.

People who are rich in money, goods, or talents need to be humble and give honor to the Giver of the gift. If we show our benefaction to all in order to receive praise and gratitude for the large amount we give, we are, in fact, giving nothing compared to the New Testament widow, of whom Jesus spoke.

> While Jesus was in the Temple, he watched the rich people dropping their gifts in the collection box. Then a poor widow came by and dropped in two small coins. "I tell you the truth," Jesus said, "this poor widow has given more than all the rest of them. For they have given a tiny part of their surplus, but she, poor as she is, has given everything she has." (Luke 21:1–4)

The rich still had plenty and enough left over to eat well, be clothed, and give banquets, whereas the widow gave everything and had nothing left to live on or to eat; she had nothing for shelter or clothes. She is the one who deserves praise for what she has done.

In Matthew 5, we read in the Beatitudes that God blesses those who are poor and realize their need of the Lord. Out of our poverty of spirit we are called to give that which God asks of us. If we are successful in our lives, we must remember to be humble so that we can still hear God's voice. It is easy to become rich in pride, in power, or in authority thus putting our trust in ourselves. When we give to others in such circumstances, it may look impressive but our soul is empty. We must remember that God shows himself to those who are humble and hides himself in the face of pride.

Actually, I don't think it is God who hides from us—God wants to be with us. It is our pride that prevents us from seeing God; it is we who have put a veil over our eyes so that we are not able to see that God is with us; God is here, we have turned our faces away.

ACKNOWLEDGING OUR GOD-GIVEN GIFTS

You need to be aware of and acknowledge the gifts God has given you. You should look for opportunities to exercise the talents you have been given and give thanks for the chance to do so. Don't be afraid to use your talents; it is by using your gifts that you show your appreciation to God for those gifts.

There is no need to hoard our gifts out of fear that there won't be enough left for ourselves if we share them with others. The Holy Spirit lacks for nothing and does not hold anything back from us. We are showered with gifts from God and, in our turn, should share them abundantly with others. As the loaves and fishes were multiplied when Christ blessed them (Matthew 14:13–21), so our talents will multiply when we ask God to bless them. We can then share our gifts with others as Jesus gave the bread and fishes to the disciples who then shared them with the crowd.

It is even harder to share a material or monetary possession with others than it is to share our creative talents. If we throw our bread upon the waters, will we really find it again after many days? It is hard to believe the quotation, "Send your grain across the seas, and in time profits will flow back to you" (Eccl 11:1).

It is difficult not to be afraid to give away our material goods to others; if we give away our last morsel of bread, can we be sure that we will get something to satisfy our own hunger? If we give away our last dollar, can we know with certainty that more money will come to us so that we can pay our next bill? We have to live in faith that if we share our possessions with others something will come to us in order that we, too, will survive.

We give our goods away and hope that, as the baskets of crumbs picked up by the disciples were more than the original amount of loaves and fishes distributed to the crowd, so also we will have more in goods, time, and talents after we share them with others. Things that we hoard will certainly wither and die; moth and rust will destroy things that we hide away, food will go bad, and clothes will become moth-eaten. What good is this to us or to others?

God delights in every detail of our lives especially as the Lord sees us develop the talents we have been given and use them in service to others. Our talents will not be perfect at the beginning of their use; they grow and develop as we practice our skills. We may stumble and make mistakes from time to time but we will not fall because the Lord holds us and guides us. Let us not be afraid to share.

WILLINGLY RECEIVE FROM OTHERS

Not only should we be willing to share what we have with others but we should also be willing to receive gifts offered to us by those around us. You may think that this would be an easy thing to do, but many people are unwilling to receive help or gifts offered to them by others, thinking that it puts them in a poor light compared to their benefactors. Perhaps it does—this is called humility and is one of the virtues to which we are called by Christ; one of the fruits of the spirit towards which we are maturing as we journey along our soul pilgrimage.

Recently, when I went out to vote, I was driving along a country road that seemed to lead nowhere, but was the direction given to the polling station. It was a road that kept me wondering if I'd missed my destination, even though I had driven this road before, I still lacked confidence in my journey. It was a road of unease and uncertainty. As I drove along, I saw a terrier running up and down the roadside and, as each car approached, the dog stopped and looked intently to see if it was its owner's vehicle.

On the return journey from my civic duty the dog was still running frantically along the road. I stopped to see if he had a tag so that I could call the owner but, though the dog was looking for help, he wouldn't let me get near him. He growled and snapped at my approach. He was a sorry looking sight and I wanted to help him, but he only wanted help from his master—everyone else was suspect. I could only speculate how the dog had become lost and what would happen to him if his owner did not come to look for him and find him.

Sometimes, this happens to us on the road of life. We may become lost and need help. However, we often have only one kind of help in mind and everything else offered to us is suspect and only worthy of our growling and displeasure. We must try to open our eyes to see new possibilities and try new ideas presented to us. Along the road of our disorientation, a new beginning is waiting for us if we are willing to trust a different direction, or the outstretched hand of God offered through a stranger.

What about your spiritual journey? Are you willing to allow someone to help you if you lose your way, your faith, or your confidence in God? Before you stray too far from the Holy Spirit ask a trusted companion to pray with you in your time of difficulty. St. Paul shows us how much he valued a praying community.

> We have placed our confidence in [God], and he will continue to rescue us. And you are helping us by praying for us. Then many people will give thanks because God has graciously answered so many prayers for our safety. (2 Cor 1:10b–11)

RECOGNIZING GOD IN THOSE WE MEET ON OUR JOURNEY

The further we walk along our spiritual way, the more we become aware that the people we meet are also on a spiritual journey whether they have recognized their pilgrimage as yet or not. We are all human beings created by God and sent to earth in order that we may proceed to our next stage of evolution. This next stage of evolution is to become spiritual beings, wholly at one with God.

When I first entered an Anglican convent in the 1960's we had a tradition that was seen by some as old-fashioned and by others as quaint or perhaps even ridiculous. The tradition expressed itself outwardly in a little curtsy as we passed one another in the cloister, recreation room, or garden. This little curtsy earned the sisters the rather ridiculing term of The Bobsy Sisters. It may have seemed silly to others but the curtsy had a deep-seated meaning behind it—the curtsy was meant to remind us to recognize the presence of Christ within the person in front of us.

When God gets our attention and we stop to look at the one we meet on our path, the chances are that we will encounter Christ in the person we see before us. In fact, God is within each person we meet and we need to remind ourselves of this constantly. The curtsy the nuns made to each other in the convent reminded them that in crossing paths with another person they were crossing paths with the Sacred One. If God presents someone to us on our path we need to take a moment, pay attention, consider the Holy One among us, and give an inward curtsy to the Christ within that person.

The next contact you have with someone on the road is a unique opportunity to meet with God in that person. You may not realize it, but the person you meet on the road may be the answer to a prayer you have made to God; or it may be possible that you are the answer to the prayer request of this same person. You need to show reverence to each one you meet on the spiritual road. Don't lose the chance to see the Sacred within the one who may seem ordinary; don't lose the chance to show that the Sacred One is present within you too. You were born in holiness and are regaining the memory of your holiness as you walk the pilgrim way.

When somebody is on your path, you must consider what is being asked of you. What is God asking of you in this situation? Are you being asked to help this person? Are you being asked to work together with this person? Are you being offered help from this person?

If someone is on the path or joins us on our journey as we walk through the day with God, then we can be sure that we are meeting this person together with the divine. We can be certain that God is relying on us to do something for this person or to receive something from her. Even if we don't like this person, even if we don't know this person, even if we can't see what possible connection there could be between us, if she is there on our path she is there for a purpose and that purpose is God's purpose.

RECOGNIZING GOD IN THE UNEXPECTED

Because of the complex nature of life these days, we have to do a certain amount of planning. There are meetings to attend, people to see, and places to go. We can't be in two places at once so we need calendars to keep ourselves organized and to ensure that we don't double book or do more than we can handle. Calendars enable us to keep our lives harmonized and in balance, making sure we even out our time of work, play, and rest.

The things we write down on our calendars are important for our day to day lives. They are appointments with doctors and dentists, meetings with school teachers and principals, or interest groups of one kind or another. Not many of us would be able to keep our family, work, and recreation events in order without one or two calendars around the house.

When we are on the spiritual trek with God, however, we should be prepared for the unexpected. We may be walking along and see something that draws us away from our planned meeting. The organized part of us may say, "Walk by on the other side; there's no time for this; keep your eyes averted; don't get involved; there are things to which we have committed ourselves."

On the pilgrimage of the soul, we have to remember that the journey is more significant than any planned events at the end of the footpath marked in the calendar square. God works in the unexpected and in miracles; God works in circular and cyclical, not so much in linear; God works in wide open spaces, not so much in small boxes.

Though the commitments we have made and the people to whom we have made them are important, our spiritual journey with God is paramount. Through unexpected happenings on our way to an engagement we may realize that God is calling us and, if we walk away in order to keep our scheduled appointments, we may miss God's call or gift to us.

So what is to be done? Any breaking of these commitments on a chance meeting on the road can only be made in prayer. We have to listen to the voice of the soul in order to make the best choice in conflicting situations.

The situation that presents itself to us on our combined physical path and spiritual journey cannot be avoided but may possibly be postponed to another time after a brief discussion and a mutual agreement with the person. If it is an emergency situation, which cannot be postponed for whatever reason, then the person to whom we made a prior commitment needs to be notified as soon as possible. In this day of cell phones and other technical devices it is usually easy to do this right away.

God gets our attention, we hear God's voice, and we become part of the great army of workers who help prepare the way for God's people to go through the gates and into the Holy Place.

> God says, "Rebuild the road! Clear away the rocks and stones so my people can return from captivity." (Isa 57:14)

> Go out through the gates! Prepare the highway for my people to return! Smooth out the road; pull out the boulders; raise a flag for all the nations to see. (Isa 62:10)

We need to be ready to do our part in smoothing out the road and preparing the highway for the safe return of God's people to the House of the Lord. If God asks us to repair the road and we don't work on it, it may be many years before someone else begins the work and, consequently, many years that people will remain in captivity, that is, in the power of "what your sinful nature craves", as St. Paul says in his letter to the Galatians chapter 5: 16.

> The sinful nature wants to do evil, which is just the opposite of what the Spirit wants. And the Spirit gives us desires that are the opposite of what the sinful nature desires. These two

forces are constantly fighting each other, so you are not free to
carry out your good intentions. (Gal 5:17)

This is captivity—being in the power of our sinful nature—hostility, quarrelling, jealousy, selfish ambition, dissension, division, envy, to name some of those St. Paul mentions in his letter to the Galatians, chapter 5:19–21. If we don't look at changing our behaviors while on our journey, the stones and boulders will remain in the road as stumbling blocks preventing others, as well as ourselves, from walking safely in God's holy path.

CONFLICTS WITH OTHERS WE MEET ON THE JOURNEY

> Spiritual existence is an endless Becoming. The whole of the mystical experience in this life consists in a series of purifications, whereby the Finite slowly approaches the nature of its Infinite Source: climbing up the mountain pool by pool . . . until it reaches its Origin.[1]

We may have conflicts or difficulties with those we meet along the spiritual journey. If we are having trouble keeping patience when we meet people who annoy us, and we really are trying to grow in patience, we may well find that we keep meeting people in whose presence we lose patience. God will cause us to go on encountering such people until we have come to a place of spiritual maturity in patience.

This is what Evelyn Underhill calls, in the passage quoted above, "a series of purifications". These purifications may come to us in very small happenings such as trivial annoyances; sometimes they are presented in large traumatic events such as major illnesses. No matter whether they are small irritations or large catastrophic events, unless we see them for what they are—i.e. opportunities sent by God to open our eyes so that we may increase in spiritual

---

1. Underhill, *Mysticism* 140.

maturity—we will remain at the same elevation on the mountain and in the same spiritual pool.

In order to advance closer to the Infinite Source we need to examine the purification events that come to us on our soul journey, not seeing them only as annoyances, devastations, or chance encounters, but as means whereby we can become closer to God and grow in spiritual maturity. The frustrations that make us annoyed and burst out in anger at someone can become a means of purification and growth when we ask God to teach us how to control our anger in such situations. We need to learn to listen to our soul's calm voice that will help us to grow in spiritual maturity during these times of purifications.

What is it that keeps cropping up in your life that makes you frustrated, angry, or impatient? What is it that makes you critical of someone, despise someone, or put someone down? What behavior in your life makes you regret your action as soon as you've done it, but still finds you reacting in the same manner again and again?

These attitudes will continue to devastate you and others until you take them into your life as means of purifications sent by God so that you can advance on your spiritual journey. Ask your soul to show you how they can be overcome with the Holy Spirit's help. This is the means whereby you can proceed along the Highway of Holiness, slowly climb the mountain, and become closer to the Sacred One.

When we come before God each day as instruments of the Holy Spirit all our happenings are orchestrated by God. If we ask to play in the orchestra of life God takes us up on our offer and all goes according to God's plan—well-ordered and in harmony. God brings into our days the people whom we can help and those who can help us. We move along God's chosen path and everything fits into place.

When needs arise someone arrives to fill what is needed. We don't bump into each other along the way. There is plenty of room for all of us to move and dance, walk and glide along God's pathways. No one we meet is without meaning to us or without some purpose in our lives. We are members of God's orchestra and God is the director of our journey. Let us make a joyful noise together with the Lord.

> Praise the Lord with melodies on the lyre; make music for him on the ten-stringed harp. Sing a new song of praise to him; play skillfully on the harp, and sing with joy. (Ps 33:2–3)

The love we see in the face of Jesus pours into our souls and from that fullness we give God's love to others. Indeed, without getting replenished at the spring of life and love, we would not be able to give to others in love. We may be able to give grudgingly, defensively, and unwillingly for a short time, thinking that every drop we give out depletes our own supply and our own inner resources, but this kind of giving is not giving in love.

When we look to the Lord for our supply, it never dries up and the more we give out the more we will be filled up. When we give love to others in Christ's name that love returns to us again. People can't help but respond to the love of Christ that they see in us. It is a sacred love, beyond this world, and people respond in the same manner.

5

Walking through Darkness and Light

LIVING THE ORDINARY LIFE

If we walk along a country road or a hiking trail we will sometimes be in sunshine and sometimes in shadow; sometimes there will be clear blue sky and sometimes clouds; we may encounter rain, sleet, or snow; at times we may get drenched and at other times we may get sun-burnt.

As we continue on our spiritual pilgrimage here, too, we will go through periods of light as well as periods of shadow. The soul will take us along the pilgrim way where trials and joys will meet up with us as we journey. On this Highway of Holiness, where we walk our soul journey, Christ will be our light along the way.

> Jesus spoke to the people once more and said, "I am the light of the world. If you follow me, you won't have to walk in darkness, because you will have the light that leads to life." (John 8:12)

What does it mean that Christ has come to be the light of the world? It means many things but most of all it means that you can count on Christ to be there to light your way when you go through difficult times.

As you go along your soul journey you don't get any special favors because you have become aware that you are on the spiritual road and growing towards spiritual maturity. You will still encounter the usual periods of darkness and light that anyone might expect in the life of a human being. The difference is that you will know that Christ is always there to shed light in dark times.

You go on living your life, trusting in the Lord's light to shine on your path; you live where you are and take the things that come to you, at this moment, whether they seem good or bad. You may think that someone else's life looks better than yours, but each person has his own difficulties and burdens to bear. The grass may look greener on the other side of the fence, but it isn't necessarily so. If you move elsewhere in hopes of finding a more pleasant land, you will have the same problems because you carry yourself with you, and people in other places have the same faults and problems as the people with whom you live and work now.

Christ's light helps you to stop focusing on the bad around you and to see the good, the riches, and the beauty right where you stand at this moment. Look around you now and find one good thing, see God in it, and thank the Sacred One for this gift to you. When you take the ordinary and recognize God in it, your perception is enhanced and the ordinary becomes extraordinary. The ordinary life lived with God at its heart becomes spectacular and reaches people so that they too come to know God and the light of Christ in their own ordinary lives.

This spiritual life is not an extra that is added on top of one's ordinary life like chocolate icing on a vanilla cake; it mingles with the ordinary life like yeast in bread dough. You do not put on and take off the spiritual life at will like a glitzy decoration, but you are, at all times, part of Christ and Christ part of you. You become one with Christ so that together you are one extraordinary being.

Christ's light shines in you and transforms your life from within. As the soul opens up to the Sacred One, you will find your ordinary life transformed into that of an extraordinary life as it shines in the light of Christ. Then, no matter what happens on the outside; no matter where you live or with whom you work; no matter if you are sick or well, rich or poor, you are at peace and you glow with a steady light bringing joy and peace to others.

HIGHWAY OF HOLINESS

DRAWN TO THE LIGHT OF CHRIST

One would think that we couldn't help being drawn to this light of Christ. What a wonderful gift to have constant light on our spiritual pathway. Why would we not want to be drawn to the light? If there is light on the path we will be able to see dangers and avoid them. Could it be that we sometimes deliberately choose to step into the dark in order to experience these danger spots? Perhaps we can't resist the temptation to try the forbidden thing; we say that it is human nature to want what is forbidden; do we think that it must be something good because it has been denied us?

When we were children our mothers may have told us not to touch the hot stove and we may have done it anyway and were surprised when we received a burn. We thought we were being denied some good thing when our mothers told us, "No". Instead, our mothers were trying to save us from suffering.

This is what Christ's light does if we let it shine on our path—it saves us from walking into danger and getting hurt. But when we are new to the spiritual journey, we may think that something pleasurable is being denied us. We may walk into the shadows in order to experience such things as illicit drugs or some immoral behavior. This will lead us on a very rocky and unpleasant way.

Of course, not every pleasurable thing is wrong and not all pleasant things cause us problems, but some will and Christ's light shows us the pitfalls so that we can avoid them. The light of Christ will never steer us wrong.

We hear the warnings but we don't always heed them. Teenagers are notorious for trying things out that they have been told are not good for them but, sad to say, many adults (Christians included) continue to do things even though they know they are harmful. Some things have bad consequences—smoking cigarettes may cause cancer, multiple sex partners can give us AIDS, and driving while drinking may kill or maim someone.

Christ does not shine the warning light to deny us genuine pleasures but to save us from disaster. The next time we are inclined to partake of forbidden pleasures, we should remember Christ's offer to shed light along our path and give thanks for its life-giving illumination of hidden dangers.

The soul interprets Christ's light and word to us and our daily spiritual practice enables us to hear and recognize the soul's voice and to follow Christ's light.

DARK TIMES

Sometimes we will have periods when we live in darkness and are unable to see our way, not because we have chosen to step into the dark but just because we have come to a difficult period in our life. This surrounding darkness may feel close and oppressive, and cause us to be afraid. We remember that we have been told that Christ has come as a light to shine in the dark world but we are not sure how to interpret this. We are still in a dark place, we still feel afraid, and we don't know what to do about it.

Christ did not pretend that we will never be in a dark place; Christ did not tell us that we will never encounter difficulties or trials. No, Christ told us that there will be such times in our lives and that Christ will be the light that guides us through those times.

If we believe in Jesus we will not remain in that darkness because light shines from Christ's presence onto our dark pathway. The darkness caused by our surrounding difficulties may remain but Christ's light will shine on it so that we can make our way through it. Christ's presence is also within us and Christ's light shines through us so that we become the light of Christ to others. Like a lantern, Christ's light moves with us, and we take the light of Christ's presence with us along the path.

The concept of Christ's light being ever present with us is a simple one and almost seems silly to say; and yet Christ's message to us is simple. We look for complicated doctrine but Christ's word was always simple and humbly expressed. We are afraid of simplicity because we equate it with foolishness. But Christ's words of simplicity are words of wisdom and truth; they are words full of light and hope; words that are easy to understand and follow.

We can expect to find God at the gateways and dwellings of the humble. Here there will always be a candle in the window and a meal to be shared. Here we should watch closely for God's appearance. We are more likely to find God's light in the hovels of the world than in palaces; in low-income housing rather than in the mansions of the rich. God is revealed in those who seek the Sacred One in the stable not the castle; God is revealed in places where people share cups of water and not expensive bottles of wine. In the gateway of the humble is where the light of Christ is revealed.

DAWN'S LIGHT

Christ walks along the path with us in the darkness and we talk with Christ as we walk together. Christ protects us from the enemies of darkness that would come upon us from the side. Christ walks by our side along the path toward spiritual maturity, keeping us company, and protecting us from these sideswipes. This is God's love for us. After a period of darkness we emerge into the light of dawn; but, whether the way is dark or light, Christ walks beside us, along the path as protector, companion, and friend.

In our turn each one of us has someone to whom we are to show God's love, be protector, companion, and friend. Perhaps we do not know who it is. Perhaps we think that we have no one special to whom we are to show God's love. Perhaps we live alone with no one to come home to and with whom to share God's love. This may mean that we have been chosen to be God's wayfarers so that we can show Christ's love and light to those whom we meet along our soul journey—those others who have no one.

The people you meet along your path are your neighbors—the people you meet at work, in the hospital waiting room, in the parking lot, on the bus, or in the classroom. Look at the next person you meet and see Christ in that person, be Christ for that person, and be Christ beside that person along the path. In this way you will start a chain of God's love and the light of dawn will grow into the light of mid-day, as it says in the Book of Proverbs. The light becomes stronger and stronger as Christ's love is shared and the flame is passed from one to another.

> The way of the righteous is like the first gleam of dawn, which shines ever brighter until the full light of day. (Prov 4:18)

GOD GUIDES EACH ONE OF US

> You are my hiding place; you protect me from trouble. You surround me with songs of victory. The Lord says, "I will guide you along the best pathway for your life. I will advise you and watch over you." (Ps 32:7–8)

God helps us and protects us in times of trouble and, as we grow in spiritual maturity, we become more and more aware of God's aid and protection. Sometimes, that help comes from other people. God uses ordinary people to help us in our time of need; and God uses us to help others when they are in difficulty. In order to help others more effectively, we are sometimes asked to go through a bad place ourselves. Going through our own time of difficulty gives us the experience and authority to guide others through their time of suffering.

Whenever we walk through bad places, we must be sure that the walk is with God and that we walk holding on to God's word. Then our feet will be steady; we will walk to the beat of God's drum, the measured rhythm that keeps us synchronized and in step with the Sacred One.

When people cannot see their way because iniquity has power over them, God may call us to be their light, their way out, and their strength. If God asks this of us we must surround ourselves with prayer and keep hold of God—we must not try to do it in our own strength.

Iniquity will present itself in our world; there will be evil; we will be confronted by and confront wrongdoing and injustice, and if we walk in God's word we will walk steadily and steadfastly, we will be unfaltering and strong in the Lord. God will provide for us a hiding place from the iniquity and evil; God will protect us from wrongdoing and injustice so that they will not have control over us. If we keep our eyes and ears on God we will be guided along the best pathway for our lives; God will advise us and keep watch over us.

In times of darkness, you will need to keep very close in prayer to God. You might say a prayer to God for guidance: Guide my steps in your word; mark my footsteps in your measured rhythm; give me a beat to which my feet can walk with purpose on the way, a beat that's steady and rhythmic, measured and strong. Guided by your word my footsteps are directed in your way; your word lights my path.

Another possible prayer is: Let no evil overcome me. Let no wrongdoing or wickedness have power over me. Let no sin have control over me; let your word be my guide and guard. Your word is good and steadies my feet. Your word is joyful and brings lightness to my steps. Your word is delightful and brings a dance to my feet.

God's word is strong, powerful, and steady; in this word you can walk steadfastly, surely, and with control over yourself, being sure that wherever the path leads it will result in some good thing, some joy, some strength, some new lesson, and some task to perform for God.

If we are foolish and walk deliberately in darkness or if we allow evil to have power over us, we will falter and our footsteps will not be sure. In darkness, without the light of Christ, we are unable to see stones on our path and we may trip and fall. The boulders come upon us unexpectedly and we slam headlong into them. Pits may be there and we could slide down into them. We become nervous and edgy, afraid at every step and every turn in the road, we are uncertain of where we will end up. At such a place and time we must call out for the light of Christ to shine on us, the light that will show us the way, and vanquish the evil one from our path.

When we walk in God's word, we don't need to be afraid of the path ahead because it is lit by the light of Christ and we know that even if there is a pit before us, there will be a way around it or through it. The way along the path will be lit with Christ's light and we will be safe on the journey.

Grow in this trust in God's light as you make your spiritual pilgrimage. Be attentive to your soul's voice that will lead you and steer you in the right way.

LABYRINTH PROMISE

Early in 2008, I went on a retreat that involved walking a labyrinth. The labyrinth was originally used in the Church in medieval times as a tool to replace actual physical pilgrimages to the Holy Land or other religious sites. Christians were encouraged to make pilgrimages to sacred places in order to gain spiritual favors but when travel became very dangerous, labyrinths served as a replacement for these faraway lands and were counted in the same way toward their heavenly journey.

Labyrinths are making a comeback to assist people to find God's guidance for their lives. The labyrinth I went to was at St. John's Anglican Convent in Toronto, Ontario, Canada. The purpose of the labyrinth walk was explained to us by two nuns who guided us on how to find God's calling for our lives by means of walking the labyrinth.

After the first evening session, I wrote in my journal, "I just came back from walking the labyrinth in the rain and evening dark, our way lit by floodlights. As I walked to the center, I repeated the words, 'Step by step I come to you, O Lord.' Then, after a while, 'Step by step I come to you, O Lord; so many mistakes but still I come.' In the center, a feeling of blessing and peace came over me. As I walked out from the center my walking pace quickened and I spoke the words, 'I am walking as if on a mission; I am sent as on a mission. Here am I, send me.'"

The next day, in my journal, I wrote, "I wonder what kind of mission God has for me. I am limited in going anywhere at present, as a recent bleed in one eye prevents me from driving and I live in a rural area where there is no public transportation."

As the nuns continued to guide us on our labyrinth retreat, Sister Elizabeth asked us to think of a symbol to explain God's guidance to us. This symbol would be used later in the creation of individual mandalas, I chose the telephone as my symbol; I realized that in this day and age, because of technology, we need not be limited in our ability to do mission work for God even if we are house bound.

My mandala consisted of a large encompassing circle to represent God and smaller circles within, representing me and those to whom I minister through telephone contact with them and in intercession for them. I added pictures of a home representing my own home from where I minister; a clock representing the gift of time that I have been given to do this mission work; a laptop computer to represent technology; and a glass dome to represent God's love and guidance that surrounds me.

In the following weeks and months, I began to do the mission work to which I had been called during the labyrinth retreat, and I felt God's guidance and love in my life.

FORGETFULNESS OF MY PROMISE

Then, almost two years after this beginning, I began to realize that things were not as they should be and I wrote about it in my journal expressing my distress at my loss of commitment to the promise I made to God at the retreat. The following passage is taken from my journal as I wrote and spoke words of sorrow to God.

I have lost a lot of what we once had, O Lord. Our relationship together has been lost because of my lack-a-daisiness. I have lost the stamina I once had; I have taken our time together for granted and not given it the priority it should have. I have let our time together slip away as if it was of no consequence; I have let go of the promise I made two years ago at the labyrinth retreat.

The life of intercession I began with such intent, I have let fall away piece by piece, bit by bit, prayer by prayer. 'It takes too long,' I said; 'I have other things to do,' I said; 'There are more important things to be done,' I said. I now confess, O Lord, that I have lost my way. I pray you to accept me back into the fold, into our special relationship, into the one and only thing that matters—the sacred bonding between us—the holy and blessed consecration of my time with you. Forgive me Lord. I would begin again the mission of intercession that I was given. I thank you for the circle of your love; surround me with your loving strength and joy.

I come with purpose and intent. My purpose is to write this book of soul journey; my intent is to tell what you would speak through me. I sit at your feet and learn from you. Show me, Lord; guide me, Lord; let me follow in your footsteps; let me follow in your way along the spiritual walk, the Highway of Holiness. The soul is faithful; it is my mind and heart that lag behind. I now receive the gift of holiness once more, I recognize God's love, and give Christ the rightful home within my being.

I have written this personal account of my forgetfulness of God and my soul purpose because I want you to be aware how easy it is for a relationship with God to slip away from you, and how important it is that as soon as you become aware of your downfall you pick yourself up again and ask God to forgive your lapse and to give you the strength to return to the Lord.

We are all pulled up short, at times, with a sudden awareness that we have let holy things slip away from us. We continue to go to our quiet place for our quiet time with God. We read the Bible, write in our journal and, one day, we realize that there is no spiritual depth in what we are doing. We are going by rote, by outward signs, but we are not paying attention—we have shut God out of the prayer process—we are in the right place but not in the right prayer presence.

I wonder why it is that we seem to go along in harmony with God for a certain length of time and then seem to back off from the search and journey. Is it because the intensity of the search becomes too much for us? Is it because ordinary life gets in the way? Is it because we are afraid of what we might become that we are so slow to evolve spiritually?

We have the desire to be with the Sacred One and we think that this desire will never end; yet, we let it go—drift away and let it slide from our grasp. We don't pursue it as eagerly as we once did; other things take priority; we hide from God's call, God's vision for us, and our spiritual vision for the relationship between the Sacred One and our soul.

How did this happen? How and when did we become blasé about such an important part of our lives? We think of ourselves as still with God but our showing up at our quiet time has become an outward shell—we, the living creatures, have left our home. We have to get back to basics.

Our soul reminds us; our soul's insistent voice calls us back to its core; "Return before all is lost," it says. God is present in the temple but we have not been full participants in this relationship. We must return and spend time, once more, in being with the God of hospitality and generosity. We have become less than whole by trying to be more—more without God—giving the Creator lip-service but not heart-service.

INNER STRENGTH

> We now have this light shining in our hearts, but we ourselves are like fragile clay jars containing this great treasure. This makes it clear that our great power is from God, not from ourselves. (2 Cor 4:7)

A relationship with God requires inner strength and the soul is where that strength lies; but the actual strength and power come from God. You must listen to the soul's voice; the soul is the container of God-essence and God-being within you. Having a relationship with God is not a fuzzy teddy bear kind of experience though, at times, you will feel a deep warm glow. A relationship with God is more than a deep happiness; it is a deep knowledge that one must follow where God leads whether it is through the desert like Moses or to the cross like Jesus; whether it is to give up riches like St. Francis of Assisi or to leave the security of Egypt for the uncertainty of the wilderness like the Israelites.

It is not always easy to be faithful in your relationship with God but listening to the soul gives you strength to go on the journey, to find your purpose, and to follow that purpose no matter what is asked of you. Along with the world, you are being led to holiness. It requires spiritual strength to be in combat with the evil one; it takes discipline to keep to your spiritual practice; it takes resolve to come running back to your inner discipline with renewed endeavor when you realize you have fallen away from your daily practice.

You will have joy in the knowledge that you are following God's call to be a contemplative without a cloister, but your soul purpose will be a purpose requiring strength and fortitude to pick yourself up when you fall, acknowledging your need of God's power and grace within you.

TRUSTING IN GOD'S PLAN

I say that I trust God's plan for me but I don't usually think of that plan as being a part of God's strategy for the whole world. I tend to think of myself as one important unit, isolated from the rest of God's scenario, and at the center of God's attention; I don't often think of God's plan for me as being a small part of a much larger whole—God's plan for the universe and creation. But, though I am only a minute part of God's plan, I am an important part of God's orchestration for all of creation to become whole and holy.

Every part of God's plan is important and if we do not each fulfill our part in God's scheme, we slow down the progress of creation towards holiness. I have tended to think of God's plan as important for me as an individual; I have thought of God as bringing me, personally, to wholeness and holiness. God's purpose for me *is* important inasmuch as if I, as one part of creation, am flawed then the whole of creation is flawed also.

God's creation is like a great tapestry consisting of each one of us fulfilling the Creator's plan in our individual lives. Without each one of us trusting and following God's plan for us there will be large areas in the universe of blank tapestry, devoid of color and beauty.

God's purpose for each one of us as individuals is important; God's purpose for each individual as part of the whole creation is important; and God's purpose for the whole of creation cannot be fulfilled until we each trust and surrender to God's plan for individual and universal holiness.

6

Expect Hills and Valleys, Rivers and Deserts

OUR JOURNEY GOES THROUGH VARYING TERRAIN

St. Peter probably said it best in his first letter: "Dear friends, don't be surprised at the fiery trials you are going through, as if something strange were happening to you. Instead, be very glad—for these trials make you partners with Christ in his suffering, so that you will have the wonderful joy of seeing his glory when it is revealed to all the world" (1 Pet 4:12–13).

When we go on an extended physical hike we will probably go through a lot of different terrain. We will find that we will walk up hills and down into valleys; we may ford across rivers by way of stepping stones; perhaps we will walk along beaches by the side of the ocean, or over desert sands with an occasional refreshing oasis.

In order to see the beautiful view over the valley from the top of the mountain, or hear our voice echo back to us from the opposite side of the canyon, we have to first climb to the top of the mountain, and this takes quite a lot of physical effort on our part.

The climb to the top of the spiritual mountain may not be easy either. It may come with fear attached. A mountain top experience may reveal itself through a trial of fire, darkness, and cloud. Moses said, "I stood as an intermediary between you and the Lord, for you were afraid of the fire and did not want to approach the mountain" (Deut 5:5a).

However, no one else can do it for you; in order to get the mountain top experience first hand you have to approach the mountain yourself; you have to go through your own trial, such as an illness, yourself; hearing or reading about it does not provide you with spiritual growth.

It is wonderful to hear second hand about the glories of God and the wonders the Lord has done for other people to bring them through their difficulties, and we are thankful to know of their experiences. But, to get the full vision of the mountain top experience, we have to walk through the fear that comes to us as part of the trial. We have to walk hand in hand with God through the fire, and step by step up the mountain path. It's not enough to hear about someone else's experiences; we have to go through the cloud and thick darkness ourselves.

Sometimes we are faced with a trial right when we thought we were on the verge of receiving some reward or success. If this happens it is difficult not to be discouraged. But God is giving us an opportunity for spiritual growth, an opportunity to climb God's holy hill and be transformed through the vision of the splendor of Christ.

Recently, a trial of this sort happened to me. The manuscript of the book that you are now reading had been accepted by the publishers, Wipf and Stock, and I was extremely excited. I arranged with them for a certain due date and I began to edit the manuscript in earnest, giving it my full attention.

Then, suddenly, I came down with a traumatic illness from which no one was sure whether I would recover or not. It was a terrible blow to me and, even though I did recover enough to leave the hospital, I was still extremely weak and knew that I couldn't possibly finish the manuscript by the date I had given the publishers.

Unsure as to whether the book would ever become a reality, I let the writing go out of my own hands and placed it into the hands of God and, through God, into the hands of the publishers. Finally, I realized that no matter how much effort I put into the work, if God was not behind it and in it, the book would have no meaning. I wrote to the publishers and they gave me an extension on the manuscript's due date, a more realistic due date, allowing me more time to do a better job than the original date would have given me.

We are given the pathway that brings us closer to God, the pathway up the side of the mountain or down into the valley, the footpath through the desert or the ford across the river. We have no choice but to walk on the pathway that God is presenting to us but we do have a choice as to whether or not we will open our eyes and see the way in which God will transform us when we willingly walk through the trial on the pathway.

We can walk on the pathway with our eyes down, discouraged, disappointed, and with blinded eyes, refusing to receive the vision God is giving us, or we can walk on the pathway with eagerness, with open eyes on Christ, seeking to find the next spiritual depth and height to which God is leading us, the deeper bonding to the Sacred One to which we are being led.

In times of difficulty, rather than planning our strategy to get through the rough times, we should rest in God's presence in peace and quietness in order to gather strength for the upcoming journey. God knows what will confront us next along the way and goes before us to prepare the groundwork. Even in this present moment God is a step ahead of us, clearing the path to make it smooth or pointing out the next boulder or chasm that needs to be avoided.

God walks each step of the way with us and will not fail us or abandon us. When the path is difficult and we feel that there is no way through, God will be there beside us to show us the footing so that we will not fall. We have to keep in mind that good will come out of present troubles. Spiritual strengthening will come out of our trials and when our faith becomes stronger we will be able to help others through their times of crisis.

The Lord prepares the way. Any boulder on the path will have a way around it and any crevice will have a bridge across it. God is with us even when we seem to be alone; we will not be abandoned.

HIGHWAY OF HOLINESS

> Do not be afraid or discouraged, for the Lord will personally go ahead of you. He will be with you; he will neither fail you nor abandon you. (Deut 31:8)

GOD'S HOLY HILL

In the Bible, we often hear about God's holy hill. We read that God lives there and that we worship the Lord there. Perhaps you wonder where God's holy hill is located so that you may go there to worship God. God's holy hill is not an actual physical place and so it is different for each one of us. God's holy hill is where we are in any given moment. Where we live is where God lives for God lives with us and abides in us. The place where we are at any given time is where God's holy hill is also. This means that at any given moment we can worship God.

We do not have to make a special trip to a special place in order to worship God, praise God, or work as partners with the divine. We can show God's love, mercy, and compassion to others, right here where we are at this moment. The place where we live or work is God's holy hill; this is the place where we worship God and where we are showered with God's blessings.

The Lord is my God. I have known this from the beginning of my life. From the time I was a baby in arms I was taken by my father each Sunday morning to the Methodist Church in Brecon, Wales. I have a recollection from when I was very young of waking up during the minister's sermon; I was held in my father's arms as he sat in the choir seats. In later years, I went to the morning service and Sunday school; then, even later in childhood and teenage years, I went to church three times on Sunday and spent many an evening during the week going to various groups held in the church building.

I was steeped in an atmosphere of a loving God to whom I spoke as I went about my ordinary life of play, school, and home. My parents never made a big deal about church and religious matters; it was all a natural part of my ordinary life. I loved to read and pray from children's devotional papers published for use at home, if I was given book certificates as gifts I would use them to buy books on spirituality—I seemed to feel a strong pull to anything that was oriented to religion and God's love—it was as if I was born with a desire to be at one with God.

When I moved away from home to go through nursing training in a big English city, I was not quite as regular in my church attendance as I was in the familiar surroundings of my home town. However, there was a church quite close to the nurses' home and hospital where I lived and worked, and I did go there once in a while and felt secure in the singing of hymns and the saying of prayers. God was there for me whenever I turned to the Lord in prayer.

The Lord is always there for us and is not only a God who does things for us when we ask (or when we don't ask for that matter), but God partners with us. We are partners in God's plan for good, partners who help to bring about God's love, joy, and peace in the land, in the part of the universe where we live. God uses us where we are today; now, at this moment.

God reveals our path step by step, in small paces. If God were to tell us what we would be doing five years from now, we would become very busy planning our route. If God were to tell us today that in five years we will work in Africa, we would spend every day from now until then planning our way, the direction that we think would get us there most easily, and we would neglect the *now* moment.

God's route may take us in unusual directions; there may be all sorts of twists and turns on our journey. Our job is not to know what we will be doing for God in five years time, or even in five minutes time. Our job is to live where we are now, to live in partnership with the Sacred One, here and now, today.

Though we cannot see what is up ahead for us, when we look back we see that our path is very much under God's guiding hand.

HIGHWAY OF HOLINESS

I know that I have strayed off God's main road many times. I have wandered away onto side roads and crescents but they have all, eventually, linked up with God's true path for me. I have learned what it is like to walk through life without an awareness of God and I have learned that Christ waits for me to become conscious of my need so that I may receive the Holy Spirit once again.

When we go off the main path on to one of these crescents, God does not abandon us, but walks with us until we realize our need for the Lord and find our way back to God. It is hard to walk on the side road where it is dark but God sends people to help us until we find the light again. When we become aware that we have hidden God's light, we trim the wick and hold the lamp high once again. We all benefit from this gift of light and find our way to the main path where we join God's triumphal procession.

The wheel turns and we get another chance. The crescent joins the main road and we rejoin the celebration of life and light. We go through the gates of Christ once more and enter God's courts. We all praise God together for bringing us to God's triumph, God's glory, and God's success. We give glory and thanks for the gift of God's light and pray that all people may be led to God and praise the Holy Trinity.

SPIRIT OF THE LAW

As we continue to walk along the soul journey, we should endeavor to hold fast to the spirit of God's law rather than its letter. Keeping a set of rules correctly to the letter will not necessarily help us grow toward the Kingdom of Heaven; embracing the spirit of the law and allowing for interpretations in special circumstances is all important.

This is what Christ did when living on earth among us; Christ showed us that one hard and fast rule cannot be used in every situation. The letter of the law is what we follow with our rational minds; the spirit of the law is what we follow in the depth of our heart and soul. From time to time, with the psalmist, we may ask God to make us walk in the path of obedience.

> Make me walk along the path of your commands, for that is where my happiness is found. (Ps 119:35)

But God does not force us to do anything against our will; God needs our co-operation and desire to walk in the way of the commandments. Requiring obedience to the letter of the law for ourselves can make us rigid and not allow for special circumstances or interpretation in differing situations; and, if we require others to keep to the letter instead of the spirit of the law, we are in danger of being judgmental of their lifestyle instead of discerning what is right for their situation.

> Then Joshua told the people, "Purify yourselves, for tomorrow the Lord will do great wonders among you." (Josh 3:5)

God asks us to sanctify ourselves so that we may be shown great wonders. God is waiting to reveal the marvels of the Creator's love but we need to have such a desire to see them that we are willing to step on to the path of obedience freely. We are seeking to know God's path for us and, knowing it, we should step onto it in faith and confidence in God. We will find happiness when we walk in the spirit of God's commandments; and these commandments are not arduous but simple—to love God and our neighbor as ourselves.

FOLLOWING IN ANOTHER'S FOOTSTEPS

When we look up and see an airplane soaring through a cloudless sky, we see that a white line like a puffy cloud trails out behind it. This cotton ball path continues to show the direction of the airplane even when the airplane itself has disappeared from view. We cannot always keep up with the sight of the plane but we can follow its trail and see the plane's course for some time. The longer the trail is in the sky the wider it becomes and after a while the trail dissipates and would be unrecognizable to anyone who had not seen the original plane in the sky. The trail joins with the other clouds in the sky and we no longer can tell the direction of the airplane.

In the same way as we watch an airplane's trail through the sky, we may begin our soul journey by being attracted to a particular person's spiritual behavior and make a good start on our own pilgrim quest by following in that person's direction. As we progress along our spiritual path, our soul increases in strength, and we begin to thrive in our faith. God shows us our own path and we make our way steadily and surely along that path, the one God gives to us.

As we continue on the Highway of Holiness, inspiration comes to us from many others with whom we meet, and we follow in directions to which we are attracted. We may also find ideas from sacred books, singing voices, and church studies. We benefit from hearing what missionaries have learned in foreign lands along their way or what aboriginal people tell us about their traditional spirituality. We may not follow these different paths exactly—we will more likely use our own sacred understanding while learning new things from their spiritual growth. We follow these trails in our own way and our God-given talents emerge in creative outpouring. God gives us gifts and calls us to use those gifts.

> God's gifts and his call can never be withdrawn. (Rom 11:29)

Gifts given to us by God and left unused by us will not be revoked but, because they lie dormant, they will waste away. It is up to us to fulfill God's calling and respond with eager desire to make beautiful the world around us with the Creator's gifts to us. By putting God's gifts to good purpose, we show our thanks to the Creator.

GOD KEEPS US SURE-FOOTED

> [God] makes me as sure-footed as a deer, enabling me to stand on mountain heights. (Ps 18:33)

God makes us sure-footed like the deer that can scale mountainsides and craggy rocks; God helps us stand firm on the heights so that we don't get dizzy and fall. When we reach spiritual heights we must keep our eyes on God and not worry about our feet. The secret to not becoming dizzy and falling is to know that God has our footsteps secure. There is no need to look down to check. God will look after our footing. Once we allow doubt of our safety and sure-footedness into our minds that is when we become dizzy and fall.

As we walk our spiritual journey, we will go through many different types of terrain. Sometimes we find ourselves on steady, straight paths while other times our path will be winding and rough; sometimes our way is mountainous, taking us up hillsides and down into valleys; sometimes our walk will be through dry desert while at other times we will have to navigate through marshy ground or even across rivers or oceans.

No matter what the terrain, we must keep our eyes ahead on God. Peter was able to walk on water when Christ called him as long as he kept his eyes on Jesus, but as soon as he looked down in wonder at what he was doing, he lost his focus and started to drown.

> But when [Peter] saw the strong wind and the waves, he was terrified and began to sink. "Save me Lord!" he shouted. Jesus immediately reached out and grabbed him. "You have so little faith," Jesus said. "Why did you doubt me?" (Matt 14:30–31)

If we concentrate on the difficult path, the height we have reached, or the ice or waves on the water, we are set for a fall. As long as we have our eyes on Jesus, on God, and on the Kingdom of Heaven, we will not fall no matter where we are on the path or how rough are the waves on the lake; no matter how high up we are on the mountain, and no matter how uneven is the pathway. We will be secure in God.

FOLLOWING IN GOD'S WAKE

When a boat goes through the water its wake goes behind it in a V shape. This shows us the path the boat is taking—the path on which the pilot is guiding the boat. This is how it is with God in our lives, even though we don't see God's footsteps on our path the Lord's guidance is still there.

We are like water skiers who attach ourselves to the boat and follow in its wake, experiencing the joy and exhilaration of the ride. And, like water skiers, sometimes we let go of the rope, lose our momentum, and fall into the water. There, like the water skiers, we tread water until the pilot of the boat rescues us. As we make our way along the spiritual journey, we follow God's path and it is a thrilling ride; we need to hold on tight and just go for it allowing God to pilot the boat and having faith that God will take us on the best path for us. If we have doubts in God's leading we let go and are bounced about by the waves of life. If that happens, we should tread water and call upon God's name until we are rescued and follow God's guidance once more.

A water skier, however good, cannot keep going at a continued fast pace but needs time to rest and recuperate, eat, and assess how far he's come. So it is with us who are on the spiritual journey; we need time to retreat, time for spiritual nourishment, and time to assess where we are in our relationship with God. This is a time to tread water, to be strengthened, to be with our pilot, and be reassured that we are on the right track— God's track.

> When you go through deep waters, I will be with you. When you go through rivers of difficulty, you will not drown. (Isa 43:2a)

For some of us, especially those of us who have not learned to swim, being in, on, or even near water can be very scary. I am such a person. I have difficulty walking over a bridge that spans a river or driving in a car that has to cross a body of water. Paddling in water at the edge of the sea or river is not so difficult because I can feel the terra firma beneath my feet. However, I don't go far from shore—I need to know that I can reach dry land quickly if I am to feel safe in the environment of water.

Sometimes, on our soul journey, we may go through difficult times. It seems as if the waves are crashing all around us and we feel at sea and seasick. At such times we must try to remember that the circumstance we are going through is God's path for us at this moment in time. On such a path God's way may not be seen because it is obscured by the waves of difficult conditions.

Nonetheless, God *is* there on the path and, when the waters are impossible for us to navigate, God lifts us up and carries us through. We may get wet, but when it is all over God our Savior will have carried us across the mighty waves so that we did not drown. We are led safely through the difficult waters to the other shore, to the new life, and to higher ground. Through such experiences, we learn to go forward to the next level of faith and trust in God.

If everything goes along easily all the time, we will not be able to exercise our faith. If there are never any times of anxiety, how can we ever increase in faith? It is so easy to get complacent and think because we are good that God will reward us with easy paths. But in order to grow in spirit we have to be willing to risk new and difficult paths; this is how we grow in faith, reach a higher plateau, and come to know God in a higher dimension.

If we look back over our time here on earth, we will remember that throughout our lives God has carried us safely over other obstacles and rocks, taken us through other streams and waves. We must remember the days of old, how God walked with us, and how we trusted in God even though we didn't know there was a pathway through our difficulties. God knew the road and led us through those rough times and God will do the same today.

HIGHWAY OF HOLINESS

> Your road, [O God] led through the sea, your pathway through the mighty waters—a pathway no one knew was there! (Ps 77:19)

We often use the words "go with the flow" but this is not always easy. We are afraid of slipping into the rushing water and of drowning in its current. But the psalmist tells us that when our foot slips God's love upholds us, and when we call out to God we will be saved. We have to acknowledge our need and as soon as we do we are saved from slipping and falling.

> I cried out, "I am slipping!" but your unfailing love, O Lord, supported me. When doubts filled my mind, your comfort gave me renewed hope and cheer. (Ps 94:18-19)

The rushing waters into which we are afraid of falling may be cares that fill our minds. When we give into worried and anxious thoughts it becomes a downward spiral that drags us into a whirlpool of despair. It is difficult to get out of such a spiral. We need to call out for help at the very beginning of such thought cycles then God's consolation rescues us and cheers our souls.

God is present with us always. This is God's gift to us. But when we ignore the gift and don't take advantage of it, it might just as well not be there. If we are drowning in a river and someone throws us a lifeline, if we don't see it or don't take hold of it, it does us no good. The same is true in our spiritual lives. When we are drowning in our cares and worries, we know that God's love is there to uphold us. But if we refuse to take hold of that love—God's lifeline—then the comfort that God offers does us no good.

We must accept the Lord's love and comfort so that our downward spiral will cease and we will be supported and saved.

KEEPING OUR EYES ON CHRIST IS TO BE SAFE

When we learn to drive a car, we are taught to keep our eyes on the road ahead and not on the road immediately in front of the vehicle. We are also told by the instructor that if we look steadily at something we want to avoid, we are likely to go toward it and collide with it. The object on which we concentrate draws us to it.

As you walk your spiritual journey, keeping your eyes on Christ will keep you safe; when you look at Christ you will be drawn to the Lord. Let Christ guide you along the way; allow Christ to take care of the how, what, and why of your next step, then everything will work out as it should. As soon as you try to take things under your own control, do things your way, and set your own guidelines, then you have worry and anxiety on top of your actual project.

If we keep our eyes down on the path instead of up toward Christ, our Guide, the obstacles will overwhelm us. When we see a hole we will fall into it; when we see a boulder we will trip over it. All this will be avoided if we keep our eyes on Christ and walk toward our goal.

When we look down and see the pitfalls we will not be able to cope. But if we keep our eyes on Christ, on the Prize, we will hardly be aware of the pitfalls. Christ takes care of them; our Leader guides us around the pit.

> Seek the Kingdom of God above all else, and he will give you everything you need. (Luke 12:31)

LOOK TO THE PSALMS FOR TODAY'S ADVICE

> Turn my eyes from worthless things, and give me life through your word. (Ps 119:37)

Sometimes the psalm verses are amazingly relevant in today's world; the verse above could have been written for today's technological age. How often do we hear the experts say that it is dangerous to watch too much television? And now the cry goes out against careless exploration on the internet, and violent video games are cited as a cause of greater violence among teenagers.

Not all television is worthless—there are a lot of good shows and entertainment. But if we find that the programs we watch are filled with violence, terrible language, out-of-control children encouraged by out-of-control adults, we have to have self-control and turn the television off or change the channel. We can choose other activities instead of watching television; we can knit or sew, we can talk to someone on the telephone. We need to turn our eyes from worthless things and look towards that which gives us life.

The same thing can happen in our daily lives. We may stop growing spiritually. We may find ourselves stuck on one channel. We seem incapable of moving off the test pattern as if our reception is not good. God tells us to move on, give another channel a chance. We need the discipline to turn our eyes from worthless things and concentrate on receiving life from God. That means we must change our outlook and adjust our antenna, so that we get better reception. God gives us life if we will receive it.

7

Finding Open Doors Along the Way

> This is the message from the one who is holy and true, the one who has the key of David. What he opens, no one can close; and what he closes, no one can open: I know all the things you do, and I have opened a door for you that no one can close. (Rev 3:7b–8)

From the very beginning of our pilgrimage journey we will find doors that open up to God along our way.

If God sets an open door before us then no one is able to shut it. God begins a creation in us and calls us to continue this work. When God opens the door, our way is made clear, and no one will be able to keep us from going through this door. No one has the power to shut it against us because God stands guard. God holds the door open and shines the Sacred light upon the entrance and along the pathway beyond.

When the door stands open we must take the opportunity to step across the threshold. God's open door will do us no good if we do not go through. Why would we not cross the threshold? Why would we not take advantage of the door that God has opened especially for us? Why would we hesitate to accept God's open door waiting for us?

Some may say they are afraid. Why would you be afraid when God is with you and guides you in every detail? Some may hesitate to put in the long hours and hard work that walking through God's open door will entail. God will be with you through this time of long hours and hard work, so why would you falter? Some may say that they are not able to fulfill such a brilliant assignment as has been given to them, but if God has given you that task and opened that door then God will complete the work within you.

God begins a new creation in us. We are to take it into our hands, walk through the gate, and know that God will complete this work in us. Now is the time to walk through the door of Christ, working with Christ to complete the task that has been given to us. If we walk across the threshold of Christ now, God's light shines upon our way, and the task we have been given will be fulfilled by the power of Christ working with us. Anyone who looks at us with spiritual eyes will see not only us but Christ, for we walk together with the Lord.

If we walk through the open door, at this moment, God's glory shines on the path and no one will be able to close the door of creativity against us.

GOD HAS A PLAN FOR US

God has a plan for us but we would be overwhelmed if we knew all that God has prepared for our future. God shows us our journeying process and the open gates for us as we go along the way. We know this is true because when we look back on our lives we can see how surely we have been guided step by step and day by day. Doors are opened by prayers that are asked and answered. As we see in the following two quotations, God opens doors in response to our prayer requests and we, too, open doors in response to God's call to us.

Jesus said, "And so I tell you, keep on asking, and you will receive what you ask for. Keep on seeking, and you will find. Keep on knocking, and the door will be opened to you. For everyone who asks, receives. Everyone who seeks, finds. And to everyone who knocks, the door will be opened" (Luke 11:9–10).

Jesus said, "Be dressed for service and keep your lamps burning, as though you were waiting for your master to return from the wedding feast. Then you will be ready to open the door and let him in the moment he arrives and knocks" (Luke 12:35–36).

The events in our lives happen as God plans. Time is all one with God. When we pray for something we open ourselves to hear God's plan. We need to pray with open hearts and minds so that we are ready to accept God's plan for us. We need to see beyond our current wants and desires. When we knock on a door, God will open one but not necessarily the one on which we knocked. We need to look around us. "I'm over here," God may say. "I was waiting for you to knock on a door, and now that you have, I'm opening this one for you."

> So much energy is wasted knocking on doors that won't open and refusing to walk through others that open to the touch. We pound on the door to certain establishments, wanting someone, the *right* someone, to open the door, invite us in, and certify us as "real" artists.[1]

God's timing and gift is not always in accord with human expectations. God's timing may seem slow to us—that is because God is patient with us, giving us time to do the best we possibly can; God's timing can be instantaneous—coming like an unexpected miracle. Things do not necessarily happen in a lateral or logical form in answer to our prayers. God *may* work that way, giving us snow when that is what we asked for; or we may have asked God for apples, shaken the apple tree violently, and then received peaches from a peach tree—a tree we didn't even know was there.

I have had experience of prayers answered in unexpected ways. For example, a few years ago, I worked on a manuscript about summer inns and lodges in the area where I lived—I did a lot of interviews and sent out the manuscript to a number of publishers but nothing came of all this work. I had worked and prayed hard for it to be accepted but it didn't happen.

Then I got an unexpected request from a publisher who was unknown to me, to write a book on prayer. For a long time, I didn't

---

1. Cameron, *Vein of Gold*, 240.

see this as God's answer to my prayer and I almost passed it up; this was a case of asking for apples and receiving peaches, and I wasn't yet familiar with this kind of answer to prayer. Eventually, I did follow through with their request and wrote a manuscript that became my first non-fiction book, "Prayer Companion", though it wasn't published by the publisher from whom I received the original request for a manuscript.

There have been open doors before me that I didn't enter; there have been times when I made hard work of it by trying to enter the wrong doors. I just didn't get it—that writing is gift not drudgery. When I finally walked through the door that God had opened before me and that I had resisted for so long—the door the Holy Spirit was presenting to me—my work was accepted.

Why hadn't I walked through the door that God had opened for me sooner? I thought that I wasn't good enough to serve God through spiritual writing. Hadn't I abandoned God on many occasions, and let God down? My refusal to accept God's forgiveness for my sins and mistakes had been holding me back. I was clinging to bitterness from past disappointments, refusing to go forward onto new paths, and allowing bitterness to paralyze my life.

When I let go of the bitterness of what might have been, my vision cleared so that I could see God's open door and I walked through that door in joy and gladness. I was set free to be with God, to sit with the Sacred One, and walk with God in pleasant paths and beautiful places.

Christ holds a gate open for you and it is up to you to walk through. When you go through the doors that God opens for you, you make progress on your sacred path toward spiritual maturity. The soul may have been showing you an open gate for some time, but the soul's voice is gentle and you need to learn to listen for its quiet sound, and become attuned to it. The way you become attuned to the soul's voice is by practicing your spiritual discipline, cultivating the fruit of the spirit, which are the attributes of the soul: love, joy, peace, patience, gentleness, kindness, faithfulness, goodness and self-control, among others.

In First Kings 19 we read of how Elijah had been rushing about in great fear; he was running from the pursuit of the prophets of Baal who he had angered in a conflict to show who was the greater God, Jehovah or Baal. Elijah traveled through the wilderness all day and finally sat down under a tree and slept. When he awoke he was fed and given water to drink by an angel, and in the strength of that bread and water he journeyed on ending up in a cave on the side of a mountain where he spent the night.

> "Go out and stand before me on the mountain," the Lord told him. And as Elijah stood there, the Lord passed by, and a mighty windstorm hit the mountain. It was such a terrible blast that the rocks were torn loose, but the Lord was not in the wind. After the wind there was an earthquake, but the Lord was not in the earthquake. And after the earthquake there was a fire, but the Lord was not in the fire. And after the fire there was the sound of a gentle whisper. When Elijah heard it, he wrapped his face in his cloak and went and stood at the entrance to the cave. (1 Kgs 19:11–13a)

Elijah had expected to hear and see God in the storm and fire and he was afraid. But when Elijah heard the gentle whisper, he stood up, wrapped himself in a holy garment, and went to the entrance of the cave, the threshold of God; here he listened in reverent awe to the quiet voice of God.

It is in the quietness that we hear God; when we stop rushing about; when we stop being afraid of the mighty windstorm; when we realize there is nowhere to go from the earthquake; when we stop being consumed by the raging fire; when we finally listen in the silence and hear the gentle whisper of God, and what the Lord is telling us, then we can go in confidence and peace to what God is calling us to do.

We have to stop creating turmoil within, be at peace, and trust in the Lord.

HIGHWAY OF HOLINESS

THE GATE OF THE LORD

In the Gospel of St. John chapter 10, Jesus describes himself as the good shepherd of the sheep and the gate through which the true sheep will enter the fold.

> Yes, I am the gate. Those who come in through me will be saved. They will come and go freely and will find good pastures. (John 10:9)

When we commune with God, Christ's gates are opened. We can enter these gates and quietly follow Christ's way to the deep center of our beings. We are led into the presence of the Lord. Here, at the gateway to our soul, is the place where we know God, the place where all paths to the Sacred One meet.

Within our soul, God meets us in a tryst. In this secret place, we will be alone with God, sing to God, and be renewed in God's Spirit through the soul's powerful gentleness.

Going through the gate of the Lord is not like entering a confined or restricted space, nor yet a walled place. We will not feel claustrophobic here but will know a sense of openness, pleasantness, and light. We will find ourselves to be at peace, quiet, and calm. We will feel light as in not dark, and light as in not heavy. We feel buoyant. The space that we are in is a new space that has been opened up—a space that has been newly created within us. It is as if we were in some sleeping state where spiritual surgery has been performed upon us. It is as if we were awake yet somnolent while the Holy Spirit worked on us and brought us into this vast open place full of God's grace.

The Lord's gate leads to freedom whether we go in or out; we find safety and protection on the path that leads across the threshold of Christ.

When you stand on the threshold of the soul and the world, you are standing at the open door of Christ. This is where the modern-day mystic stands; she is free to go in and out, bringing the pains of the world to be healed at the door of Christ; taking the soul essence, in the form of prayer, to heal the world.

Standing firmly on the threshold of the open door, which is the Christ, the mystic holds the gentle power of the soul and offers it to the world through prayer for healing and holiness, for the sacred wholeness of the world.

The soul's shimmering facets portray all that is your life; all that your being has navigated in this life; all that you have suffered and overcome; all that you have enjoyed and shared; all that has made your soul and your being stronger and more sacred is revealed through the mystic's gentle soul qualities and used for the healing and sanctity of the world.

BALANCE IN LIFE

There is a balance in life of advance and retreat, of activity and rest. Christ is the gate, the threshold over which we cross to go in and out of the world. We go out to do God's will; we come in to rest in Christ. Each time we cross this threshold, it is in the name of Jesus. We go through the gate of Christ to perform God's works, and we return through the same gate to rest and renew the strength of our souls.

Advancing and retreating, we work in Christ's name and renew our spirit in God's Holy Name. We never leave Christ's presence but rather live within Christ and Christ within us. Christ is the gate, the open door; Christ is our whole life.

We come in and out of Christ's gate freely, advancing and retreating, yet never leaving the threshold of the very Christ. Work and rest, advance and retreat, are two sides of the same gate, the same threshold. The gate is Christ and the threshold is Christ.

> Open for me the gates where the righteous enter, and I will go in and thank the Lord. These gates lead to the presence of the Lord, and the godly enter there. (Ps 118:19–20)

The door of Christ is the threshold of the soul. When you cross this threshold in prayer, through the door of Christ, you enter into a relationship with God—a sacred connection between God and the soul. Jesus encourages us to stay living with him so that we will become spiritually fruitful.

> Remain in me, and I will remain in you. For a branch cannot produce fruit if it is severed from the vine, and you cannot be fruitful unless you remain in me. (John 15:4)

SEEK GOD'S FACE

> The one thing I ask of the Lord—the thing I seek most—is to live in the house of the Lord all the days of my life, delighting in the Lord's perfections and meditating in his Temple. (Ps 27:4)
>
> My heart has heard you say, "Come and talk with me." And my heart responds, "Lord, I am coming." (Ps 27:8)

Sometimes we think it might be nice to get away from the world and dwell in the house of the Lord all our days. Perhaps we have spent time in a silent retreat in a monastery and it felt good to think of being away from our problems forever. For most of us this isn't going to happen and, in any case, a monastic life has its own set of difficulties.

As one who spent sixteen years of my life in a convent as a professed nun, I can tell you that people who live in a monastery or convent still have to contend with their own faults and those of others. The act of entering a religious order does not make one perfect no matter how much one desires to be so; one still has to go through the rigors of life in order to grow in spiritual maturity.

The psalmist hears God tell him to come to the Lord and talk with God; the psalmist's heart responds that he is coming. We may desire to seek God's face in God's house or to behold God's sacred beauty in a convent; but God asks us simply to come and talk with the Lord where we are now—no props, no special place, and no special privileges. We are contemplatives without a cloister; God calls us to come and talk with the Sacred One and we respond that we are coming; we don't have to have a special permit as hermits did in medieval times, all we need is a heart that desires to be with God.

God is not exclusively in a particular religious building. God is not in one priest only, one nun, or one holy person; God is everywhere and lives in each one of us. It is our job to seek the divine in the place where we are at this moment. God is here with us. We must look at our situation to see how God desires to be with us. When we seek the Sacred One, we will find God. The very act of seeking God causes the Lord to appear because coming and talking to God acknowledges that God is already present with us.

COMING TO A CROSSROADS

In the book of Acts, chapter 9, we see Saul actively persecuting Christ's disciples. He was sincere in doing what he thought was God's work and God, knowing his sincerity, came to Saul in a light so powerful and overwhelming that he lost his sight for three days. Saul would never forget his powerful conversion.

God knew that Saul's temperament could be used to God's glory and to the advancement of the New Way. Once Saul had seen Christ in a vision, heard Christ's voice, and talked with Jesus, God was able to use Saul's bluster for good, to further God's Kingdom. Saul stopped persecuting the Christians and became one of Christ's apostles himself.

This was a crossroads in Saul's life. Saul saw the face of Jesus on the road to Damascus and he suffered three days of blindness following this vision. Then Ananias, a follower of Christ, was instructed by the Lord to go and heal Saul of his blindness. He went to Saul, laid his hands on him, and Saul regained his sight. After this Saul was baptized and made a commitment to follow Christ with all his heart. He stopped persecuting Jesus and his followers and became a follower of Christ, giving the same zeal to this as he had once given to the persecution of Christ's disciples.

HIGHWAY OF HOLINESS

From time to time we come to a crossroads. It is a time and a place of decision-making as to which way we are to proceed on the road of life. Perhaps some possibilities present themselves but we are uncertain which way to turn. This is a time of waiting upon God; of listening to Wisdom as she calls out to us, whether from the hilltop or the gates leading into the town; it is a time for us to examine God's call to us.

> Listen as Wisdom calls out! Hear as understanding raises her voice! On the hilltop along the road, she takes her stand at the crossroads. By the gates at the entrance to the town, on the road leading in, she cries aloud, "I call to you, to all of you! I raise my voice to all people." (Prov 8:1–4)

The way may not have been revealed to us as yet, but will clearly open up for us in time. We have to be patient and not rush into anything, until the direction is apparent. This is the creation that is being prepared for us—brought to the moment of birth by the Father, awaited by the Son, and inspired by the Holy Spirit.

We should use this waiting period as a time of preparation so that we can ready ourselves as fully as possible for the upcoming road. The Holy Spirit will move across the face of the waters and our life's calling will be revealed. In the womb, in the dark cocoon of our transformation, the Creator begins the newborn work in us, continues the sacred work in our souls, and prepares us for the makeover.

Wisdom waits beside the new life, before and behind, encircling us with her strength and presence. The Holy Spirit hovers aloft to bring forth the new creation. The Triune God inspires, transforms, and guides us; and our direction at the crossroads will be made clear to us by Wisdom.

TAKE CARE NOT TO SILENCE GOD'S VOICE

> The Lord says, "I was ready to respond, but no one asked for help. I was ready to be found, but no one was looking for me.

Finding Open Doors Along the Way

I said, 'Here I am, here I am!' to a nation that did not call on my name." (Isa 65:1)

Sometimes we silence God's voice through neglect. We listen to the voice of our rational mind but forget to go deeper and listen to the voice of God as God speaks through our soul. We put a lot of effort into looking for what would be good for us to do next but we forget to stop and listen to what God has planned for us to do next. We forget to look at the graph of our life tapestry to see what colors God wants us to choose for our soul's beautiful creation.

At one and the same time the pattern for the next stage of our soul's canvas is simpler and more complex than what has been done so far. As we get older our lives become less complicated because we get back to basics. We see things as they are presented to us and we hear things as they are told to us without putting a spin on them. Despite the fact that our lives are less complicated, we have gained knowledge and wisdom over the years, and we are willing to try more demanding tasks than we did when we were younger. We still use the same tools to perform our new challenges and so simplicity is at the core of any new project God asks us to take on.

The tools of the spiritual life are trust, faith, prayer, love, joy, peace, and patience. These are the seeds that come from the harvest of the Spirit. As we gather the fruits of the Spirit we keep some seeds from the crop to plant in the next spring season of the soul. If we are in the season of winter, we allow the field to lie fallow so that the soul can rest and regain its nutrients by listening to God's word and taking in the essence of God's grace.

If we pay attention during this time of renewal and transformation, God will show us the next part of the graph for the tapestry of our souls. The Sacred One will help us find the right colors, the right textures, and the right tools to proceed to our next stage of beautiful soul work. God is ready to respond to us but we have to ask; God is ready to assist us in our spiritual transformation but we have to seek the way of the Lord.

HIGHWAY OF HOLINESS

Sometimes we wander around not knowing what to do. Our time is wasted because we flit from one thing to another; we haven't found our own calling, our own city in which to dwell. We are desperate to find our niche; we are spiritually and creatively hungry and thirsty. We are not fulfilled.

If you are in a situation like this, you need to ask the Lord to show you what it is you are to do. You need to be shown your vocation and recognize it, so that you can be fulfilled, live abundantly, and be satisfied. You need to be open to God's leading. The way for you will be made clear as you try new things even if they seem risky. That is how you grow, by taking risks; that is how you come into your fulfillment, by going through the open gate in front of you and following the path ahead of you.

The path leads you to the city or place God has prepared for you, the place where you come to live in fulfillment. You are led along the path, step by step, and along this path you are delivered out of your distress because you trust and follow where God leads.

> Some wandered in the wilderness, lost and homeless. Hungry and thirsty, they nearly died. "Lord, help!" they cried in their trouble, and he rescued them from their distress. He led them straight to safety, to a city where they could live. Let them praise the Lord for his great love and for the wonderful things he has done for them. (Ps 107:4–8)

If you are lost and you ask for direction, God will lead you on the right path. If you follow, Christ will bring you into your own land. When you arrive in your own place, be sure to give thanks. You may be inclined to think that this can't be your path; that the path you've been shown is much too brilliant for you. But God's paths are always more glorious than we could ever imagine for ourselves. God gives more than we could ever ask or imagine. Once we have set ourselves on God's path, then we can watch out for wonders to be revealed.

OPENING YOUR HEART TO GOD

> Joyful are those who listen to me, watching for me daily at my gates, waiting for me outside my home! For whoever finds me finds life and receives favor from the Lord. (Prov 8:34–35)

All things come to us in God's time and that time is made possible when we sit peacefully waiting and watching for God at Wisdom's gates, opening the door of our hearts to the Lord. When we open the door of our hearts we begin to understand the depth and breadth of God's love for us and the lengths to which God will go to bless us with grace and generosity.

8

Continuing on the Soul Journey

LOOKING OUT the window this morning I see growth abounding everywhere. Soft green tips of new growth show at the ends of the trees' branches; the peony bushes have grown, imperceptibly, by six inches in just a few short days; the holly bush has sprouted delicate soft new leaves. This is how our spiritual growth progresses—it is imperceptible, inevitable, and continually new.

Sometimes, in nature, the new growth gets beaten down by rain; delicate leaves get eaten by foraging deer; sturdy plants get trampled by a bear. But, when the distressing time has passed, we see that the plants regenerate themselves.

In our spiritual development, also, new growth may be vulnerable in times of difficulty or doubt; in times of illness or pain; in times of loss and bereavement. But our spirits, like plants in nature, will recover, rejuvenate, and regenerate when the time of distress has passed; our spiritual growth will be stronger in its re-growth than it was in its first growth—as a plant that has been pruned produces stronger branches and better fruit than when it grew untamed.

> Dear brothers and sisters, I close my letter with these last words: Be joyful. Grow to maturity. Encourage each other. Live in harmony and peace. Then the God of love and peace will be with you. (2 Cor 13:11)

Continue on your spiritual pilgrimage, journeying day by day, and keeping your soul open to receive nuggets of God's love along the way. Suddenly, a new insight may come to you and, just as suddenly, you may reject that insight because it is beyond your spiritual understanding at that moment. The soul, however, will grasp that nugget and keep it protected deep within. Later, when that same insight is presented to you again, you will recognize it as a gift from God. You will accept it, perhaps tentatively at first; you will look at it carefully and examine it, to see what treasure it is that God has given you.

Some insights are given to us by God many times before we have reached a point on our soul journey where we are able to recognize God's truths and receive them whole-heartedly using them for God's glory and the healing of the world. God is patient with us and doesn't give up after one or two tries; in fact, God never gives up at all. The soul, in partnership with the Sacred One, accepts these gifts, keeping them as in a cocoon until our spirits have matured enough to understand the meaning of God's insights given to us. Then, transitioning like butterflies, they emerge into the sunshine of their day, and God's gifts are set free to work in the world for God's glory.

GOD AT THE CENTER

The soul journey and spiritual pilgrimage is the walk with God at the center of our lives. God leads us along the Highway of Holiness, drawing us step by step to run after the Sacred One. We have to take care that we do not allow ourselves to become the center or object of the pilgrimage. It is possible to think that we are doing such great things, making such great strides, and reaching such great spiritual heights, that we begin to see ourselves as examples of extreme saintliness for all to follow.

The thing is that if we think that *we* are doing great things, reaching great spiritual heights, or being extraordinarily saintly then none of this could be further from the truth. It is not in *our* ability to achieve any of these things; all holiness and spiritual growth is of God's doing and gifting. If we *have* reached great spiritual heights along our journey it is most likely that we will not be aware of it, and will certainly not brag about these things, or draw attention to them.

In order to avoid the pitfalls of false pride on our soul journey we need to live a balanced life. Prayer, as we have said, is extremely important but, if we focus on prayer to the neglect of mental and physical activities, we become out of balance and begin to think of ourselves as someone amazingly holy and capable of doing marvelous things—more like a magician than a saint.

If we work with our hands—gardening, cooking, sewing; work with the intellect—reading and writing; work with creative arts—painting, carving, and drawing; if we employ ourselves in the work of the body and mind, joining work with prayer and prayer with work, we become balanced, rounded people—spiritual, physical, and intellectual beings—God working in us and us working in God.

Saint Benedict taught that work is prayer and prayer is work. This is the balanced life—the spiritual, intellectual, and physical intertwined, as we see in the life of Jesus Christ here on earth. The true spiritual pilgrim is focused on God and has God at the center of all her works.

LIVING A FEAR-FREE LIFE

Some people live their lives in constant fear; I know some who live in fear of dying and fear of living; fear of pain and fear of not sleeping; fear of being alone and fear of living with others. I cannot imagine living in that kind of constant fear. In order not to be filled with fear we have to be filled with and surrounded by God's loving peace and light. When a person is filled up with God's love there is no room for fear.

The answer, then, is to fill your being with God's love, to draw from God's fountain of love and light, and to discard any fear that comes and immediately replace it with love. If you sweep your being clean of fear but then leave it empty and void, there is room for other fears to rush in; nature cannot bear a void. When your being is cleansed of fears, God's love and peace must be taken in immediately. That is what prevents fear from rushing back in to your being. Love leaves no room for fear, love fills every corner of your being with light and life, and there is no room for fear to enter, expand itself, and torment you.

It is not enough to empty oneself of fears for then the heart, mind, and soul stand empty waiting for the next fear to rush in. Having emptied oneself of one's current fears, one must then draw in God's love to replace those fears. Filled with God's love there is no room for fear to return; fear cannot abide in God's essence of love; fear cannot live next to God's love.

There have been times in my life when I have been fearful but as I take in God's love there is less and less room for fear. If I have a fear-thought, I immediately ask God to fill me with love. I ask God to fill my mind, my soul, and my heart with love's blessing.

As you go along your spiritual journey, growth in knowledge of God's love will help you overcome a life of fear.

CHILDREN IN CHRIST

In his first letter, John addresses Christ's followers as children. About the time we become teenagers we don't like to be called children anymore. We want to be seen to be grown up and to be given the privileges of those who are adults. As we get older in years we often wish that we didn't have all the responsibilities that come with adulthood—we may long for those times when we were young enough to be protected by our parents; and may wish we could once again cry in their arms and be given a healing kiss when things go wrong.

John addresses the Christians to whom he is writing as children because they were new in the faith and needed to be shown this amazing religion of love. Christianity was not merely a matter of keeping minute rules of behavior but a matter of living a life of love and growing in spiritual maturity.

At first interpretation, Christ's way of love may seem easier to follow than a religion that is filled with strict rules that have to be carefully kept. The reason that the Christian way of love seems easy at first blush is that we see ourselves as the happy recipients of the love of Christ. We receive love and understanding from others when we have strayed from the path, we receive forgiveness from members of the congregation when we have sinned, and we are assisted by others when we are in need.

Eventually, of course, we realize that we, as members of this religion of Christian love, are not only recipients of that love but are also called to be givers of love and understanding to those who have strayed, givers of forgiveness to those who have sinned, and helpers to those who are in need.

Like teenagers who want to be adults because they think it will be easier to go their own way and that of their peers than to follow strict rules handed down by parents and society, new Christians may be surprised when they too are called to be doers of the Christian love as well as glad recipients of it.

John reminds us that it's not enough to *say* that we love each other—we have to show the *truth* of that love by our actions (1 John 3:18). How do we show love of Christ toward others? It is by putting others before ourselves; it is by understanding others' needs; and it is by forgiving others instead of being judgmental. God's way of love is one of simplicity and humility.

In Christ's life on earth we see Jesus showing love through an understanding of others. Christ is able to empathize with others; Christ is able to feel other people's hunger, pain, and disease; Christ sees the daily struggle of the poor, the sinners, and the sick; and Christ sees the ones who should be helping them—the Pharisees, the Elders, and the Priests—as using their religious laws to make themselves look good and to make excuses for not helping others. Christ never stopped trying to point out to the religious leaders their misunderstanding of the law and the misinterpretation of the importance of their own station.

We need to ask the Lord to show us the way and direct us on the path of simple love. God is in the small things, in quiet walks, and restful places. Let us not overwhelm others with guilt and judgment; let us surround ourselves with a peaceful and restful aura where all can find the love of God.

The spiritual pilgrimage runs parallel to the journey of the physical, intellectual, and emotional. It moves more slowly and, at times, intertwines with it. The body, mind, and ego run headlong towards their peak and, having arrived at the glory years, they sit there waiting for the end of time, perhaps declining into memories of what once was.

The spiritual journey paces itself, steadily moving forward, knowing that time is on its side. In fact, the spiritual way is timeless, continuing on after the death of the physical, mental and emotional part of our being, going forward into eternity. We continue on the spiritual pilgrimage throughout our life on earth, even if we think we've gone as far as possible in our spiritual maturity.

TRANSFORMING INTO SPIRITUAL BEINGS

The soul is the home of the essence and grace of God. The soul continues to expand within and around the body as it proceeds along its journey. The soul is our very being, holding the essence of God, the essence of grace, the essence of spiritual qualities that shimmer as they continually grow in maturity and holiness.

As our physical cells continue to grow and expand—renewing themselves—the old dying off, the new coming to life, so the spiritual cells joyfully come to life within the soul. The spiritual fruit matures, the soul qualities become stronger, as we are transformed into the next stage of evolution.

The Creator transforms the caterpillar into a butterfly, the seed to ripened fruit, and the human embryo to a mature spiritual being. God desires to be at one with all creation; and God desires to bring humanity into close spiritual ties with the Creator; human beings are continually being transformed more deeply into spiritual beings so that they might become one holy being with God.

As we proceed further and further along the soul journey, along the way of transcendence, of transformation, and of purification, we become closer and more at one with God in the uniqueness and depth of our relationship with the Sacred One, walking our way back to the Creator from whom we first came to this earth.

GOING THROUGH DIFFERENT STAGES OF THE JOURNEY

Each reader of this book is at a different stage of the soul journey and therefore the way in which each person will continue on the pilgrimage will depend upon where you are at this present moment.

As there are different stages in one's journey towards union with God, so also there are different ways of living out the spiritual life. Over the two thousand years since Christ came to earth, there have been numerous ways in which God's vocation has been heard.

Many are called to follow and serve Christ in what might be considered an ordinary life—a Christian family life of one woman married to one man, bringing children into the world and having these children baptized into the Christian way of life.

Nowadays, families are often scattered far and wide across their country or even across the world. People move to new places to follow their line of work or the spouse's line of work. I traveled to Canada from the United Kingdom when I was in my early twenties to follow a nursing career and many others have done similar things.

Since the birth of Christianity, people have lived single lives, married lives, and family lives; they have lived lives as missionaries, lives as monks or nuns, lives as anchorites or beguines, lives as teachers, nurses, or doctors.

In the late twentieth and early twenty-first centuries women have had more life-style and work choices given to them than in the previous centuries, not all of which have been easy choices. In this day and age, women are able to work in areas of physical labor, join the military life, or climb to the top of the business world.

Women may go out to work while men may choose to stay at home to look after the children; in many families both husband and wife go out to work while the children may go to a day care center during the day or stay at home with a live-in nanny to look after them.

Our choices of Christian living are many and varied, not necessarily making for easier decision-making. Varying shift work hours, for instance, can make daily prayer time extremely difficult to plan and extremely easy to let go.

So, at the end of this book, we find ourselves coming back to its beginning where we awoke to a spiritual need within ourselves, a desire to become less frantic in our daily lives, and a yearning to find a relationship with God. We long to live less stressful lives and we yearn to be more peaceful within. We search to grow in maturity of spirit, to connect with our soul, and be filled with the grace and essence of God.

Throughout our lives we continue on toward spiritual maturity and, at times, it seems to be a struggle. It is not that we don't want to be with God—we do, but life gives us so many options and sometimes it is difficult to choose the right one. So, again, I would urge you to put a short time aside each day to be with God in order that you don't lose sight of the joy of being at one with the Lord.

PRAYER FOR THE JOURNEY

Lord, I am yours. I desire to grow into one holy being with you as my center. I long to be with you; I thank you for your gift of grace; I thank you for your desire to be with me. Help me to be open; help me to expand my being so that I can receive more and more of you into my soul's center. Feed me your spiritual nourishment so that I can grow in order to receive your wondrous grace. Let me be a peaceful place where people can rest in you.

Post-Script

During the writing of this book, I have found myself becoming the person I believe God is calling me to be—a contemplative without a cloister; through the writing of this book, I have begun to discover the presence of my soul within me and around me and am discovering the soul's importance in my spiritual journey.

While I have been writing and praying this book, I have become aware that soul is not just an alternative word for spirit, but is a spirit-filled entity within and around my being. My soul is filled with the Godhead, at one with Christ, and overflowing with the essence and grace of the Sacred One.

Through the reading of this book, I pray that you will find the contemplative in you and discover that you can live the life of a contemplative in the world without a cloister. I pray, also, that you will find your holy soul within your being and know her voice. I pray that you will know God indwelling your body and transforming you into a spiritual being as you travel on your Soul Journey along the Highway of Holiness.

Bibliography

Baldwin, Christina. *Life's Companion: Journal Writing as a Spiritual Quest.* Bantam Books, 1991.

Cameron, Julia. *The Vein of Gold: A Journey to Your Creative Heart.* Jeremy P. Tarcher/ Putnam, 1997.

Doyle, Brendan. *Meditations With Julian of Norwich.* Bear & Company, Inc. 1983.

Maguire, Nancy Klein. *An Infinity of Little Hours: the trial of faith of five young men in the western world's most austere monastic order.* New York: Public Affairs, Advanced Reading Copy, 2006.

Myss, Caroline. *Entering The Castle: An Inner Path To God And Your Soul.* FREE PRESS, A Division of Simon & Schuster, Inc. 2007.

O'Donahue, John. *Eternal Echoes.* Perennial, Imprint of HarperCollins, 2002.

Underhill, Evelyn. *Mysticism.* Digireads.com, 2005.

www.ingramcontent.com/pod-product-compliance
Lightning Source LLC
Chambersburg PA
CBHW070921160426
43193CB00011B/1550